my mother
in memoriam

manolo's

new shoes

drawings by manolo blahník

The Monacelli Press

contents

When I was approached to do a second volume of my sketches my immediate reaction was, 'Oh no, not again!' But then, two minutes later, I thought to myself, 'Why not? If what has for me become a way to relax is entertaining to others….' Sitting at a table surrounded by pencils, inks, brushes and papers has been a source of pleasure for me since my childhood, in the same way that the poems of Don Federico García Lorca have constantly inspired me throughout my life. As a child, when I couldn't sleep, my mother used to read Lorca's verses from *Romancero Gitano*, or her own favourite 'Romance de la luna, luna', to me and my sister (very beautifully, I must say – with perfect, rhapsodic intonation). The words that make up Lorca's verses are as fundamental to my work as the tools that I use for the drawings which ultimately form the basis of my work.

MANOLO BLAHNÍK
London, 2010

'Romance de la luna, luna'

La luna vino a la fragua
con su polisón de nardos.
El niño la mira mira.
El niño la está mirando.
En el aire conmovido
mueve la luna sus brazos
y enseña, lúbrica y pura,
sus senos de duro estaño.

-Huye luna, luna, luna.
Si vinieran los gitanos,
harían con tu corazón
collares y anillos blancos.

-Niño, déjame que baile.
Cuando vengan los gitanos,
te encontrarán sobre el yunque
con los ojillos cerrados.

-Huye luna, luna, luna,
que ya siento sus caballos.

-Niño, déjame, no pises
mi blancor almidonado.

El jinete se acercaba
tocando el tambor de llano.
Dentro de la fragua el niño,
tiene los ojos cerrados.

Por el olivar venían,
bronce y sueño, los gitanos.
Las cabezas levantadas
y los ojos entornados.

¡Cómo canta la zumaya,
ay, cómo canta en el árbol!
Por el cielo va la luna
con un niño de la mano.

Dentro de la fragua lloran,
Dando gritos, los gitanos.
El aire la vela, vela.
El aire la está velando.

FEDERICO GARCÍA LORCA
For English translation, see page 198

8

From his elegant persona to the delicate, almond-toed shoes he designs, the word that encompasses the world of Manolo Blahník is 'fastidious'.

It applies as much to the impeccable, coconut-white suits, worn with the grace he learned from his Spanish mother, as to the sculpted shoes, poised on slender heels, designed when he arrived in London from the Canary Islands more than four decades ago.

I have so many personal memories of Manolo Blahník moments – starting with cherry-ripe fruits hanging from green suede platform shoes made for designer Ossie Clark. That was when London's King's Road was hip and happening and this new cobbler's shoe box of a store was at the end of a rainbow of colourful, 'swinging sixties' clothes shops.

My head is filled with images of leopard-print slippers, garnet-red plush mules and narrow ankle boots lined in sable or lapped in lace. I can see Bianca Jagger gliding gracefully on platform soles; and Sarah Jessica Parker, so pregnant that I cannot even imagine how she balanced on her stilettos, while giving Manolo an award in New York.

Yet, most of all, I prize rare glimpses into a design soul. These have given me a deeper understanding of an aesthetic that is so powerful and unique that 'Manolo' is up there with 'Marlene', 'Marilyn' and 'Jackie', among the single-word immortals.

I love listening to Manolo swooping from one cultural reference to the next, talking in a single breath about 'Balenciaga, Zurbarán, pom-poms and tassels – where I come from'; and then, clasping a crystal-embellished slipper, saying, 'Ah Sissi, poor Sissi!', referring to the star-crossed Austrian empress, whose very name brought tears to the eyes of Manolo's rigorous Czech father.

You can see the designer's personal journey in the shoes: feathers blowing in the wild wind of Africa that lay across the water from the family's banana plantation; the lace-and-silk of Iberian culture, absorbed from the rich paintings of Velázquez; or the Palermo of Visconti's *The Leopard*, an ode to crumbling Sicilian splendour.

But only he can explain his boyhood stirrings of fascination with shoes, as he sat in an early movie house. The first flashes were after watching Maria Montez in 1940s gilded kid oriental shoes in *Ali Baba and the Forty Thieves*; then Marlene Dietrich 'triggering incredible desire' by dangling from her toes a slipper wafting with marabou feathers; Anna Magnani creating 'a moment of great sexual tension as she shakes the sand from her high-heeled shoes'; and 'Monica Vitti lying on a bed in *L'Avventura*, ecstatically pulling up a nylon stocking'.

The current fetish for overtly sexualized shoes, caging the foot or binding it on a vertiginous platform, cannot have surprised Manolo, even though his own approach is infinitely more subtle and romantic.

The shoe designer – who is the heir to such legendary names from the past as Andre Perugia and the mysterious Belle Epoque shoe maker Yanturni – once told me why he thought sensuality was the essence of footwear.

'Hands are exposed all the time but feet are prohibited,' he said. 'That is why there are orgasmic moments when a shoe comes off. Deep down I can see the reason that shoes are sex objects and why shoes and stockings have always been linked with masculine arousal.'

With delicacy, elegance and grace, Manolo has moulded the sensual shoe, caressing it into shape. Spotted as a fresh talent at the start of his career by the inimitable *Vogue* editor Diana Vreeland, the Manolo Blahník name is now associated with shoes that have become more than *objets d'art* or, as he puts it, 'objects that happen to be in fashion'. He has created the essence of female fantasy and male adoration.

SUZY MENKES
Fashion Editor of the *International Herald Tribune*

11

africa

12

13

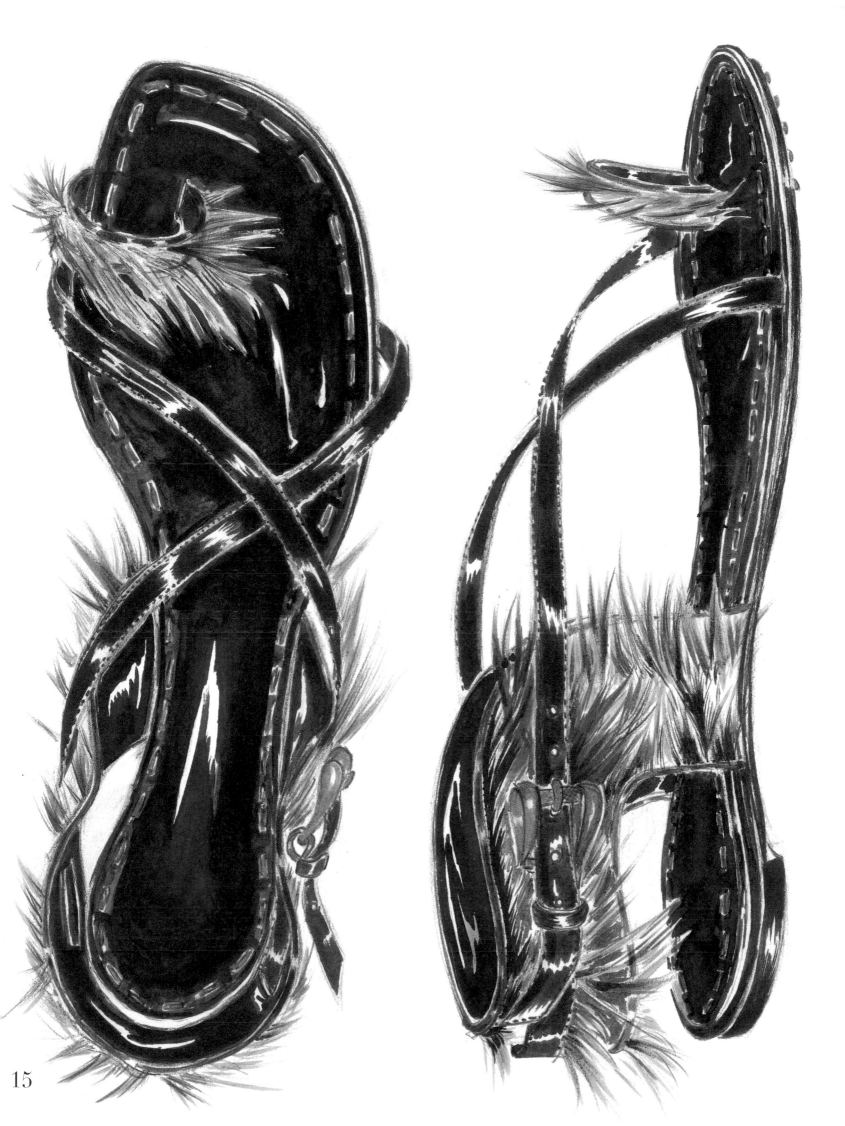

18

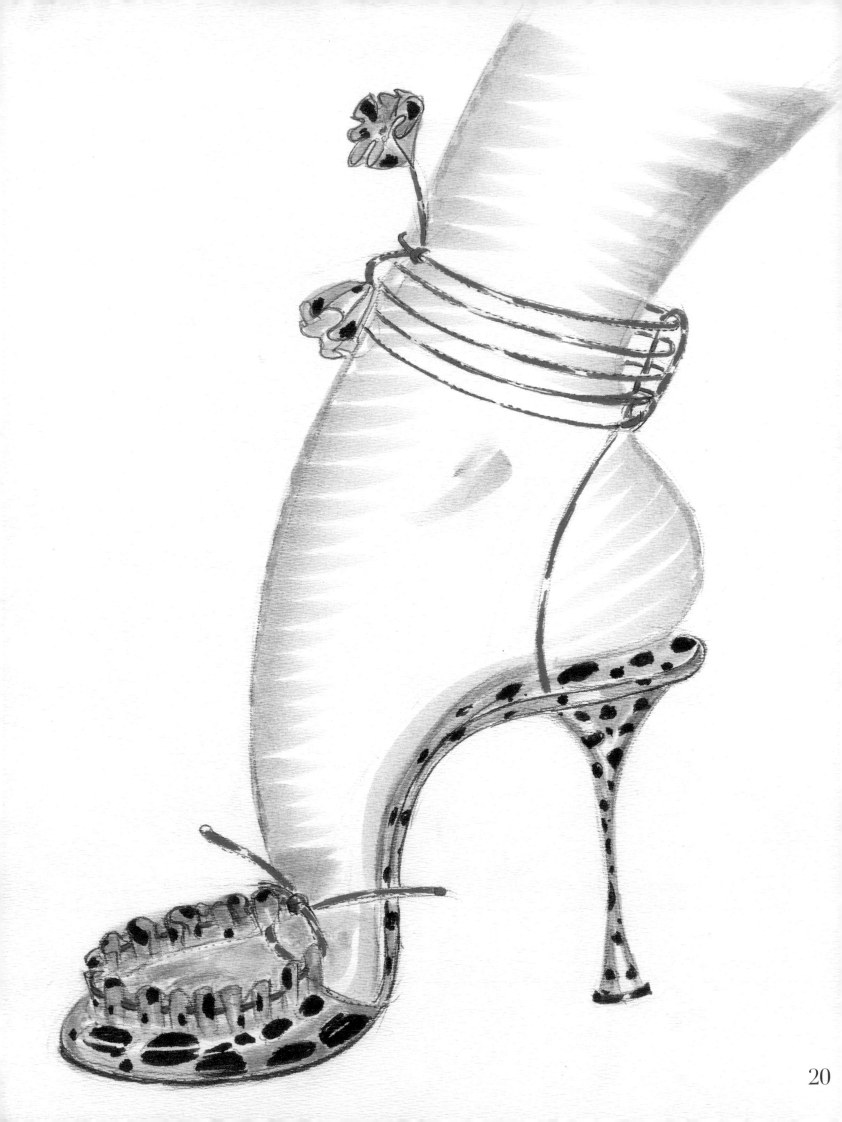

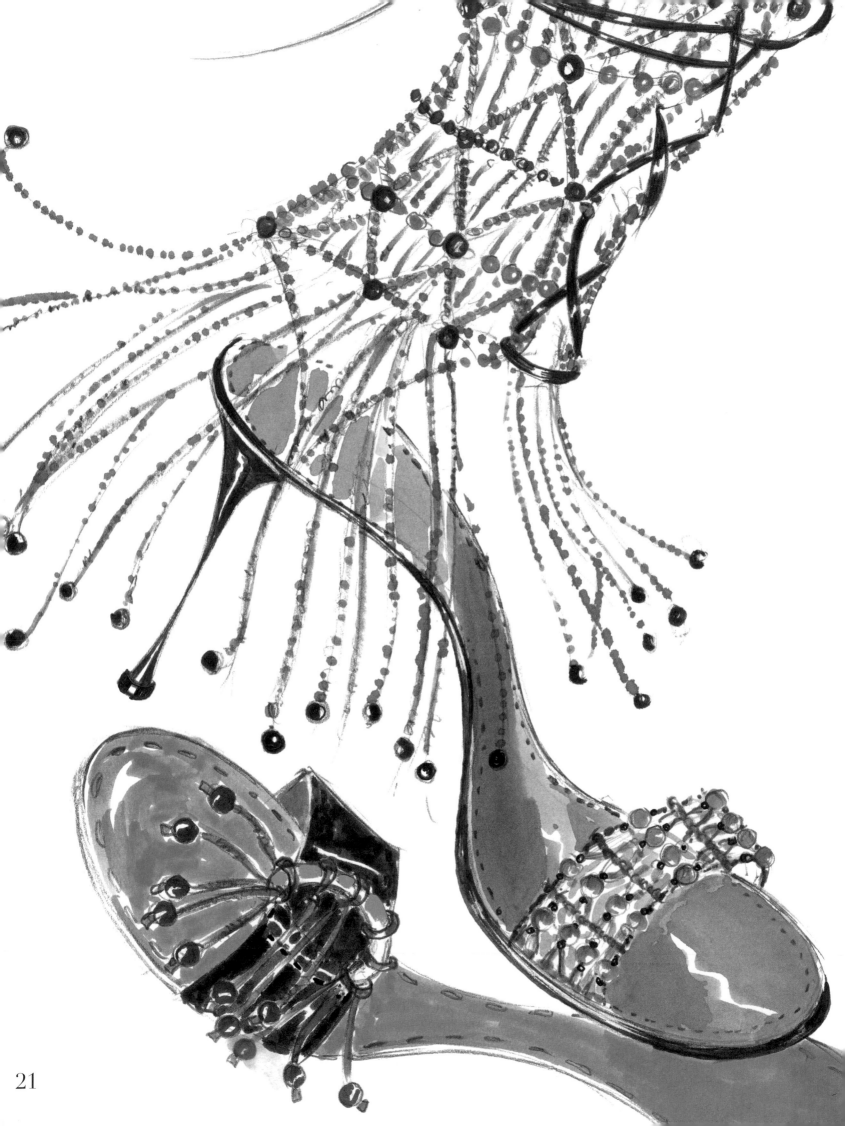

pleats

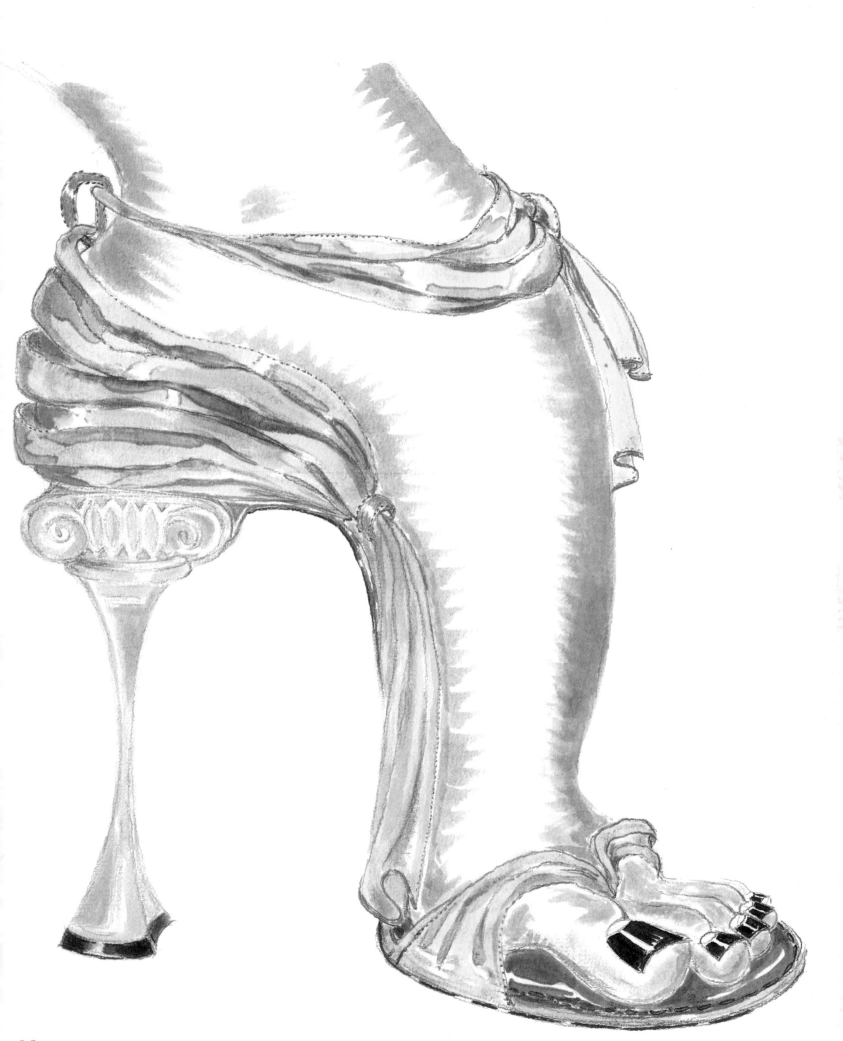

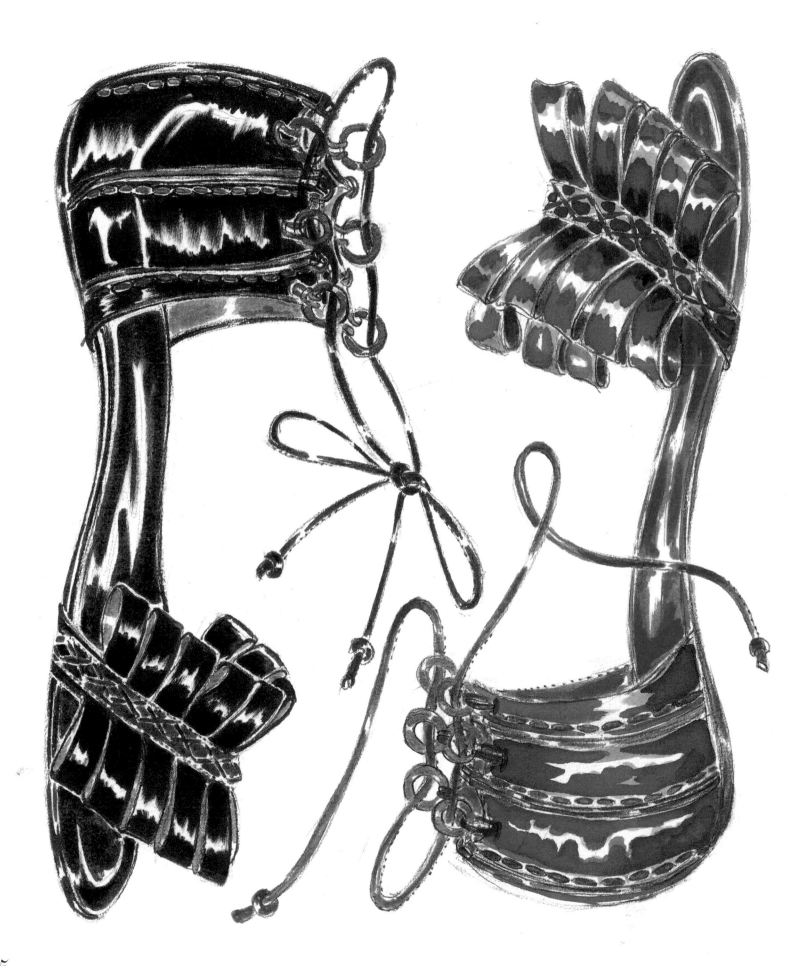

Dear Manolo...

I just wanted

to write and

tell you how

much our family

loves your

shoes....

with licks

and kisses

Grace

VOGUE

GRACE CODDINGTON
Creative Director

meow!

meow!

Bart always
wears his "Kenyattas"
to the beach...

Bart also
takes them
to Africa when he
goes on safari.....

meow!

meow!.

meow!

Purrrrrr

and Pumpkin likes
to look after "Mothers" Kenyatta's
when we are sitting in front
of the fire and dreaming
of summer time ....

meow!

meow!

...but when
we go to the
office, Pumpkin
prefers something
with a bit more
of a heel .... like
my other all time
favourites "Cameranas"...

meow!

... which work for a party too...

THE CONDÉ NAST PUBLICATIONS INC.   4 TIMES SQUARE   NEW YORK, NY   10036   (212)286-6151

35

spain

38

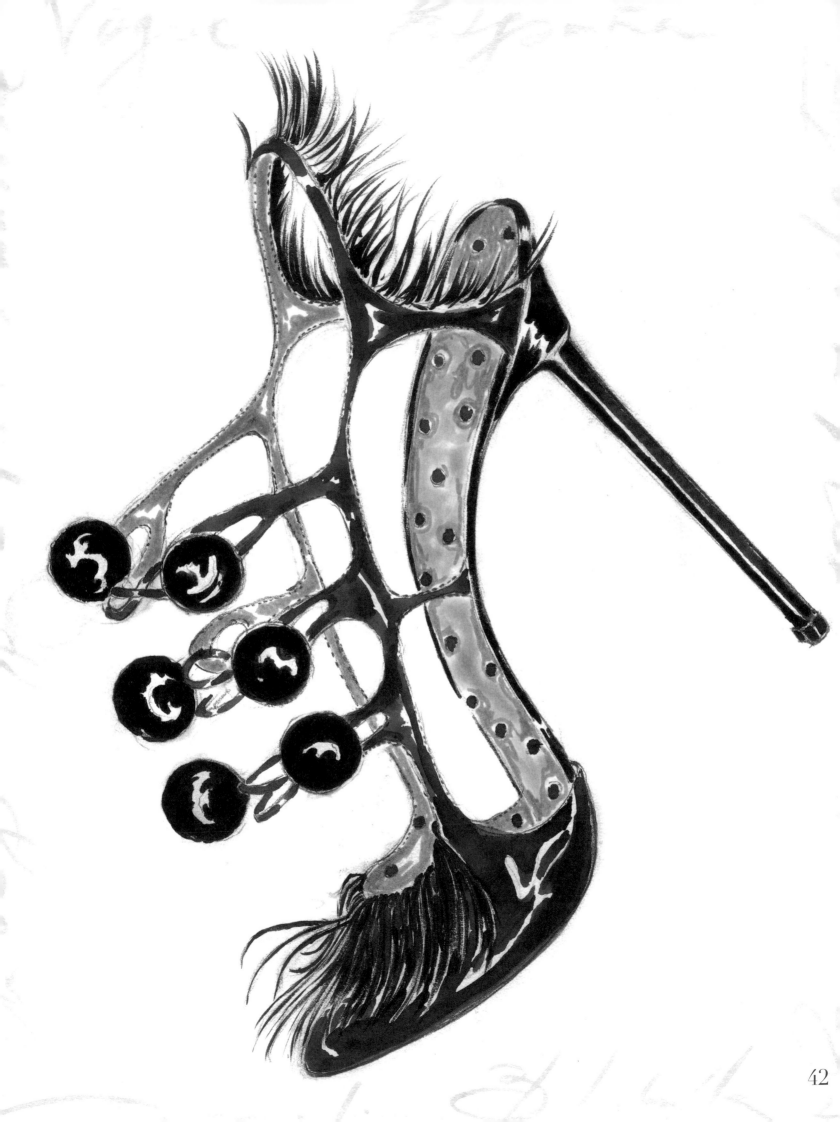

THE SPANISH SIDE OF MANOLO BLAHNÍK

The thing that surprised me most about Manolo Blahník when I first met him twenty years ago was how Spanish he was. I had expected that his Swiss upbringing and his life among the international jeunesse dorée of the 1960s and 1970s would have erased the Hispanic roots of his childhood on the island of La Palma.

I would certainly have found that quite understandable in someone who lives in England and is constantly travelling worldwide for business purposes. And even more so when he has such an un-Spanish-sounding surname as Blahník.

Although I have become familiar with his great love of Spain over two decades, it never ceases to surprise me every time I see him or when he calls on a weekend from the farthest-flung places on the planet and asks me, with an air of homesickness, what's happening in Madrid. He reminds me of those people who have had to leave their homeland for political reasons – although that is not the case for him – but who never stop thinking about it from their place of exile and dream only of going back. To Manolo, whose work prevents him from returning as often as he would wish, Spain has become something like the Promised Land.

It is also a very catholic love that embraces everything from the court of the Habsburgs to Pedro Almodóvar, including *cocido madrileño*, Lola Flores, the art of the Spanish Golden Age, Federico García Lorca or Renaissance religious sculpture. It also embraces our former colonies, reaching from the Philippines to Cuba, via Mexico and the Argentine. Although Manolo seems to remember little of what has happened in the recent past, he still has a prodigious memory when it comes to the movies of La Faraona or María Félix, for example. And he can perfectly recall the songs that the maids used to listen to on the wireless as they did the ironing every morning at his home in La Palma.

I remember that in the early 1990s he came to give a talk for the summer courses at the Complutense University of Madrid and we went on a trip to the monastery and palace of El Escorial, built by King Philip II, which Manolo had not visited since his childhood. Suddenly, he surprised both me and a few passers-by with an impression of a long-forgotten singer, Blanquita Amaro. That was everything in a nutshell: the elegance of a black-clad royal court and a life lived between outer walls of granite and inner walls of whitewash and *azulejos*, the paintings of Velázquez and Zurbarán and, moments later, a blast of Cuban dance music.

But I believe that the thing that best sums up Manolo's love of Spain is that, of all the international honours and awards he has received throughout his career, the one that thrilled him most was the Gold Medal of Merit in the Fine Arts, presented to him by His Majesty King Juan Carlos of Spain in 2002. This and having designed the shoes that the Princess of Asturias wore on her wedding day at the Almudena Cathedral in Madrid.

CARLOS GARCÍA-CALVO
Fashion Editor of *El Mundo*

form

47

49

structure

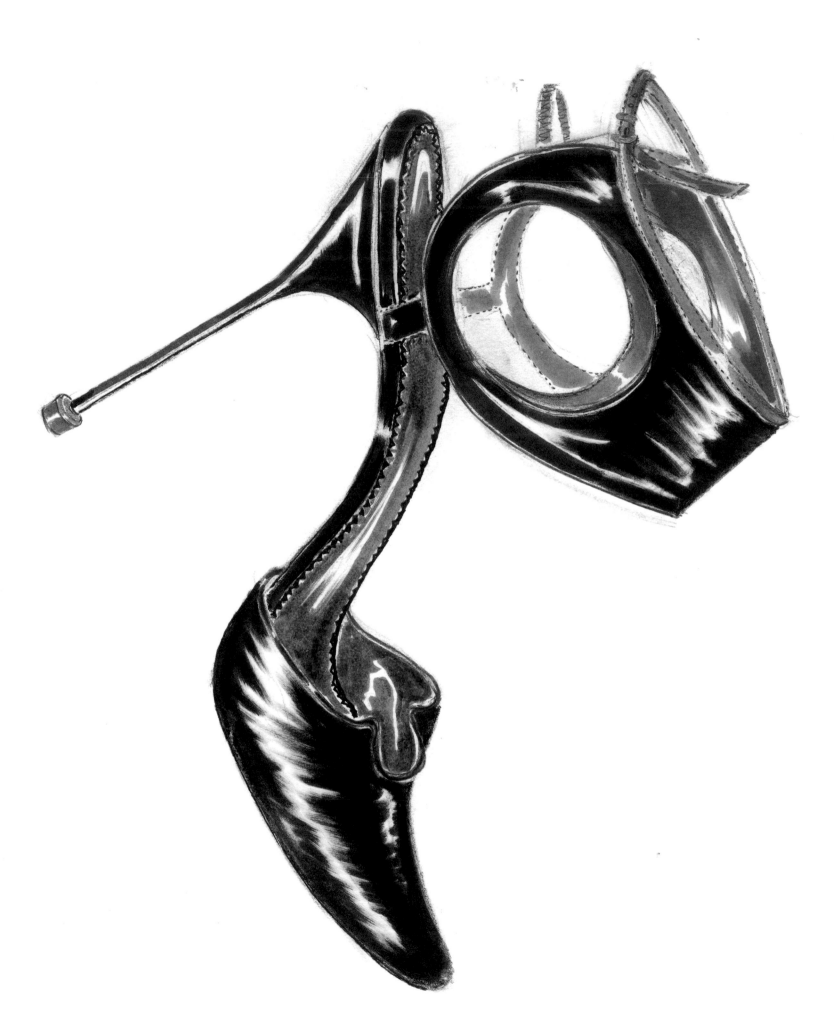

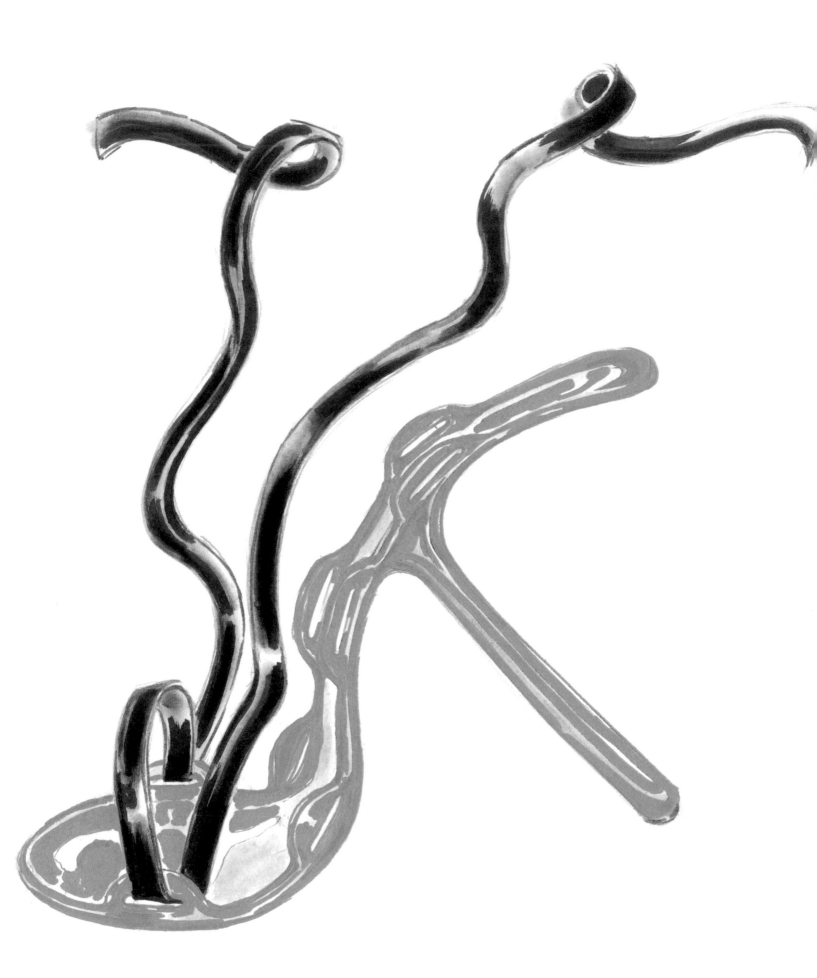

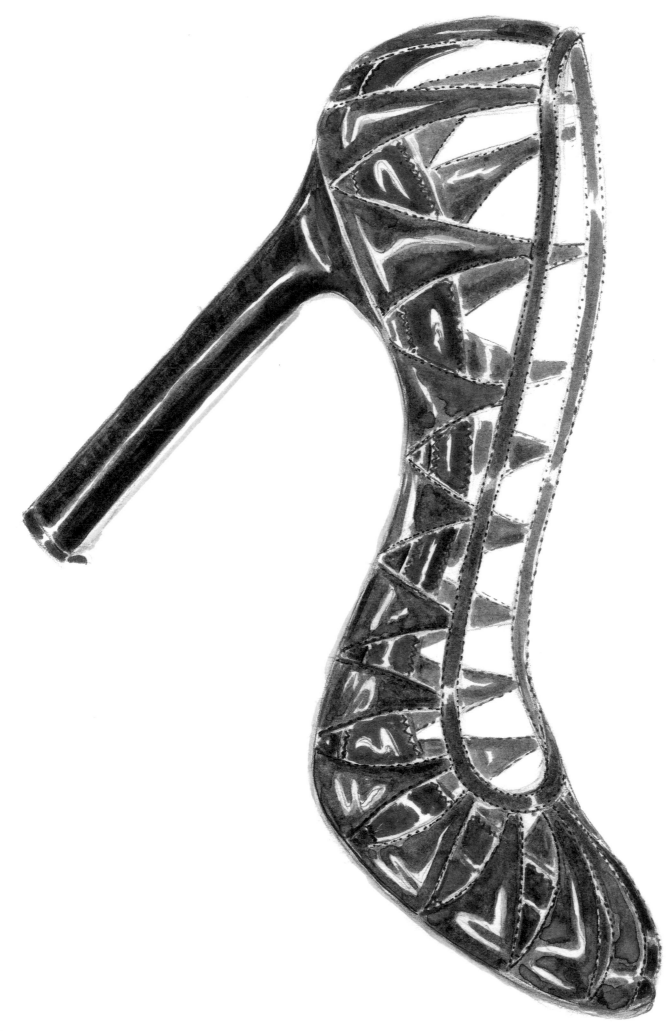

equestrian

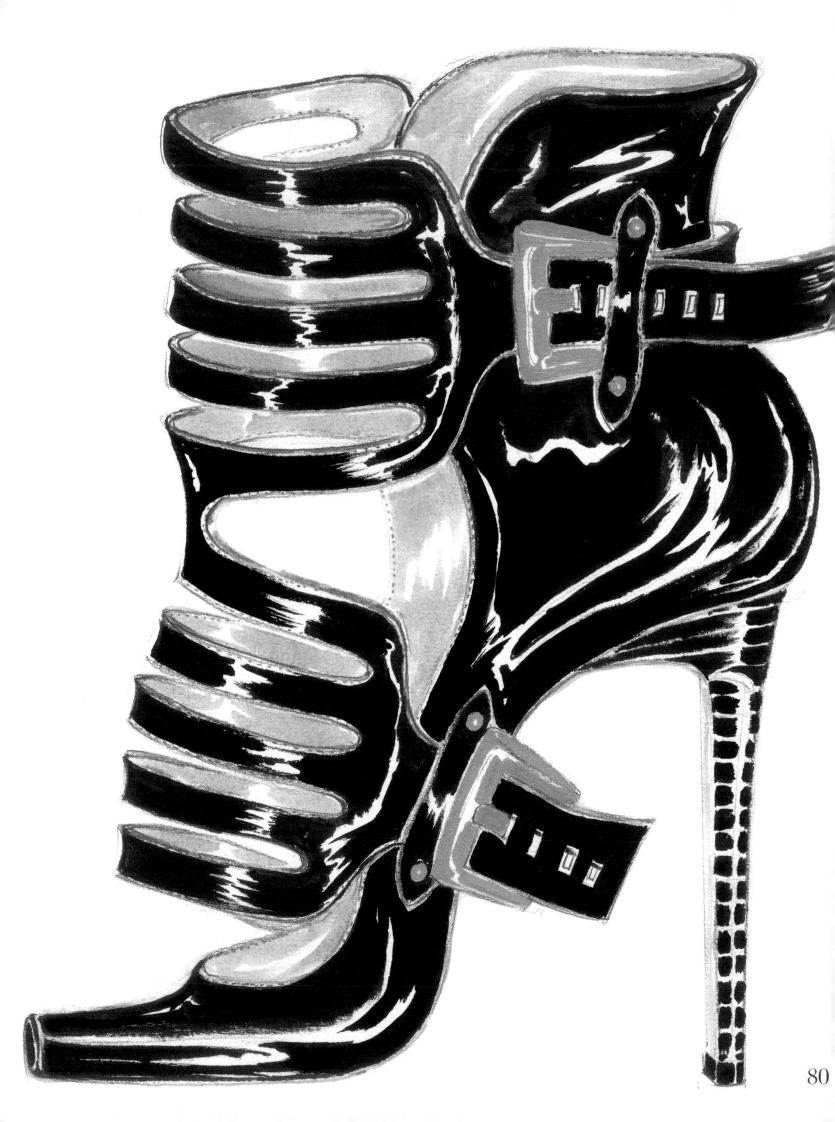

82

nature

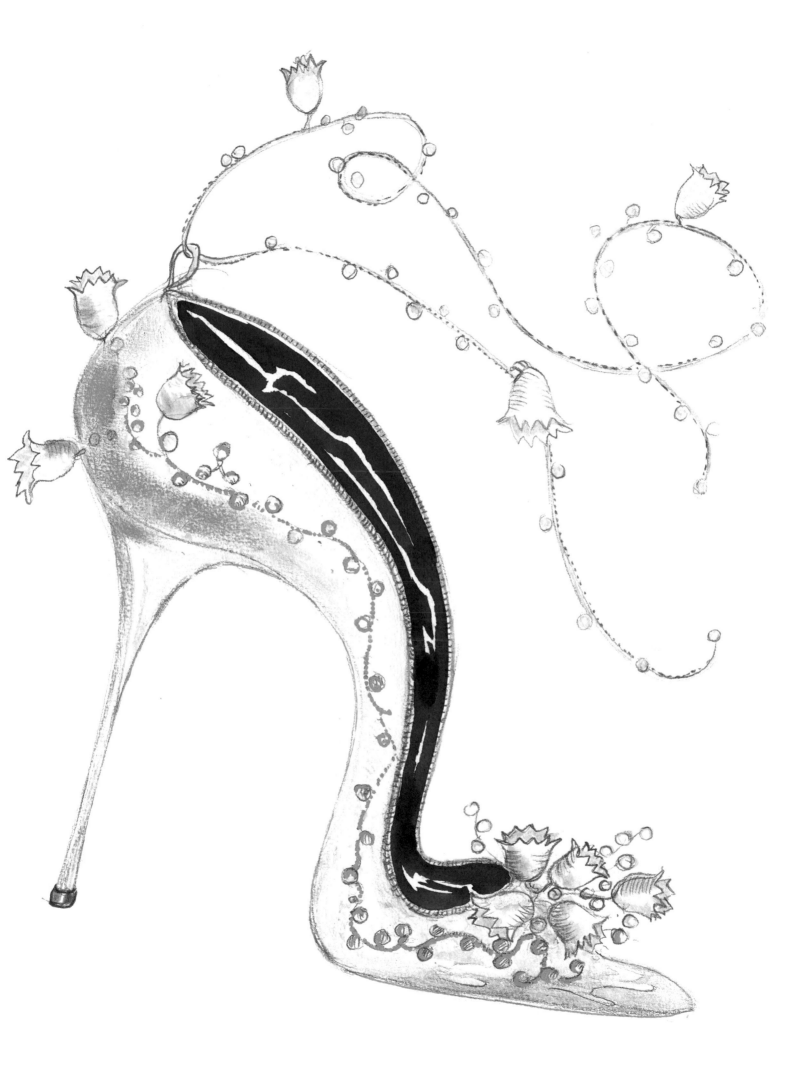

botany

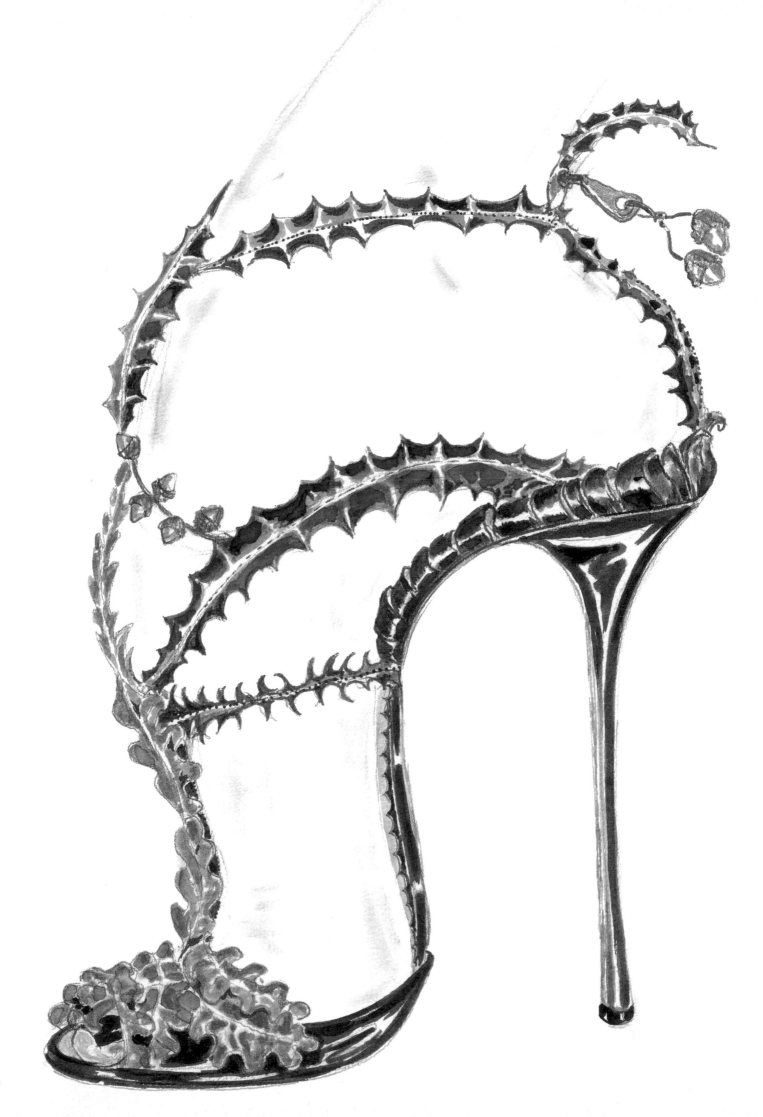

94

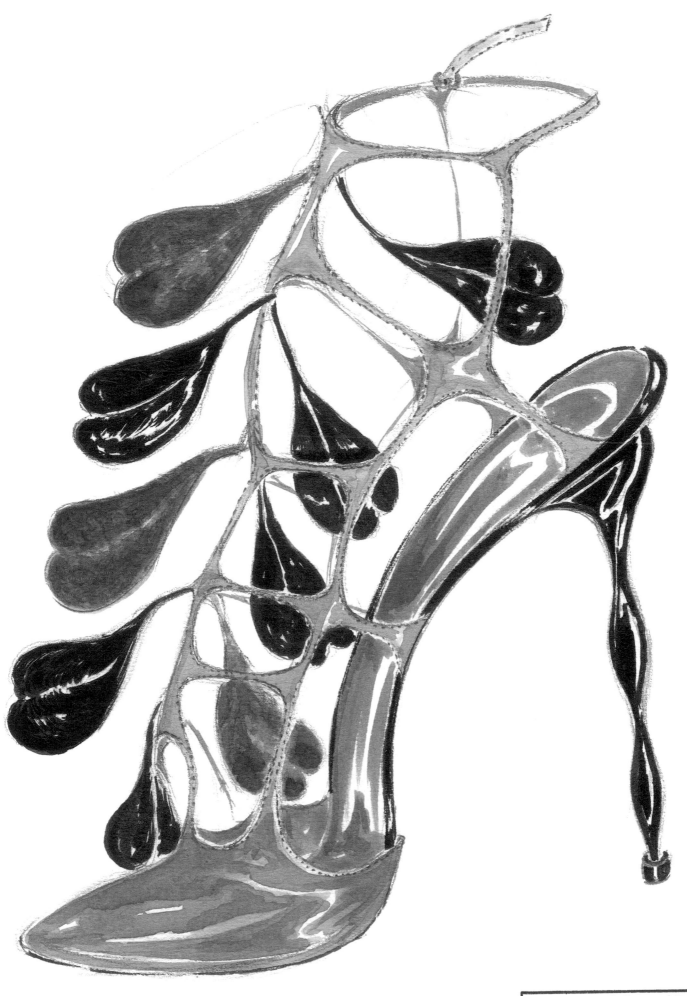

95

marie antoinette

When someone asks me about how I design costumes, I say that a look for a character starts with the head and ends with the feet. But when I think of Manolo's beautiful shoes, I start with the feet and go all the way up to the head. I have been a fan of Manolo forever. I believe in shoes. I cannot understand when an actress, to be comfortable while shooting a close-up seduction scene, takes off her shoes and puts on flip flops. Manolo creates characters with his shoes. Not just beautiful and elegantly designed, his shoes are also comfortable. One can wear them without feeling one is doing a trapeze act. When I was asked by Sofia Coppola to design the costumes for her movie, *Marie Antoinette*, I had the perfect opportunity to work closely with Manolo. I suggested to Sofia that we should contact him to see if he would be interested in designing and making the shoes for Marie Antoinette, played by Kirsten Dunst. Sofia thought it was a great idea, but would Manolo? Manolo liked the idea. His input into the movie was very precious. One got a sense of lightness, elegance and extravagance, as well as humour. There is a sequence in Sofia's movie when we see how M A is becoming terribly fashionable. We had Manolo's shoes there, as main props, because no one can be more fashionable and extravagant than a lover of beautiful shoes. In the opening sequence a lazy M A is eating cakes while a pretty maid puts a delicious shoe, which Manolo made for us, on her mistress's foot. With her choice of music for the sound track, Sofia sets the mood of her movie. It was such a pleasure working with Manolo. Manolo and his team are always so supportive and I am grateful to be connected with his creativity whenever possible.

At the moment I am doing three *Tosca* productions: at the Met, in Munich and at La Scala. Guess what? Tosca wears beautiful Empire-inspired Manolo shoes!

MILENA CANONERO

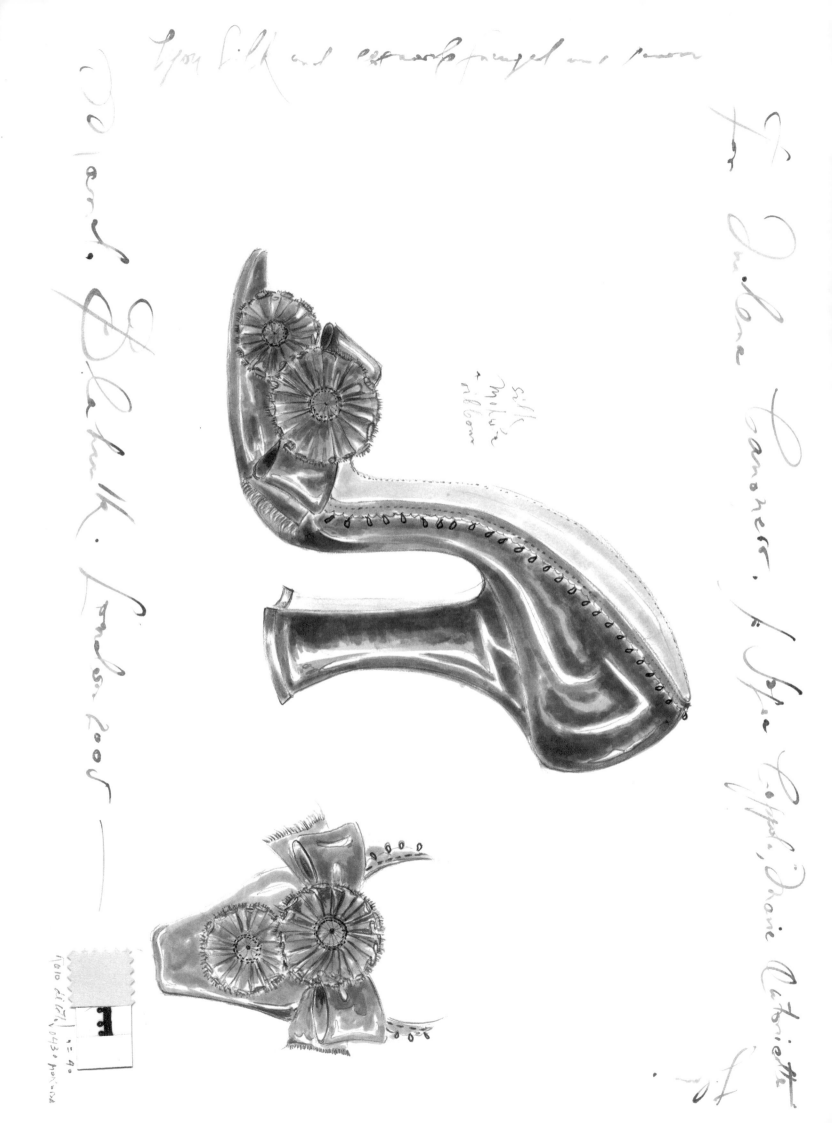

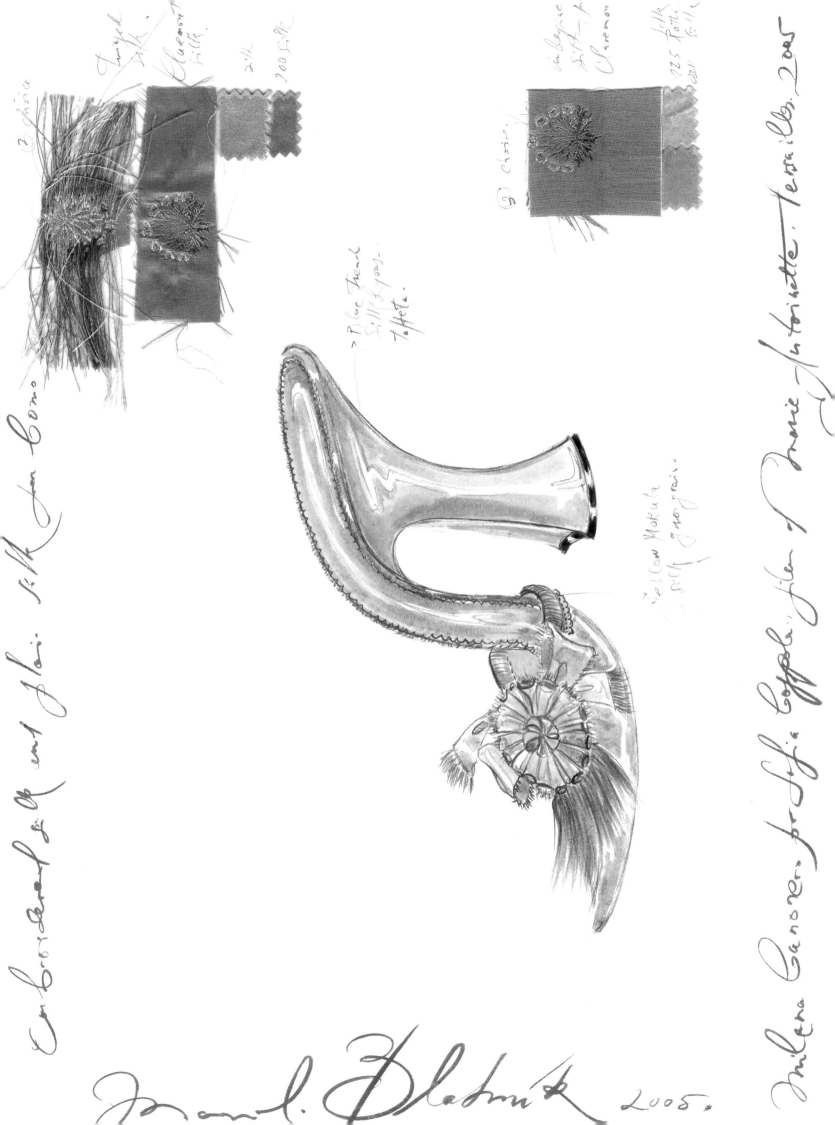

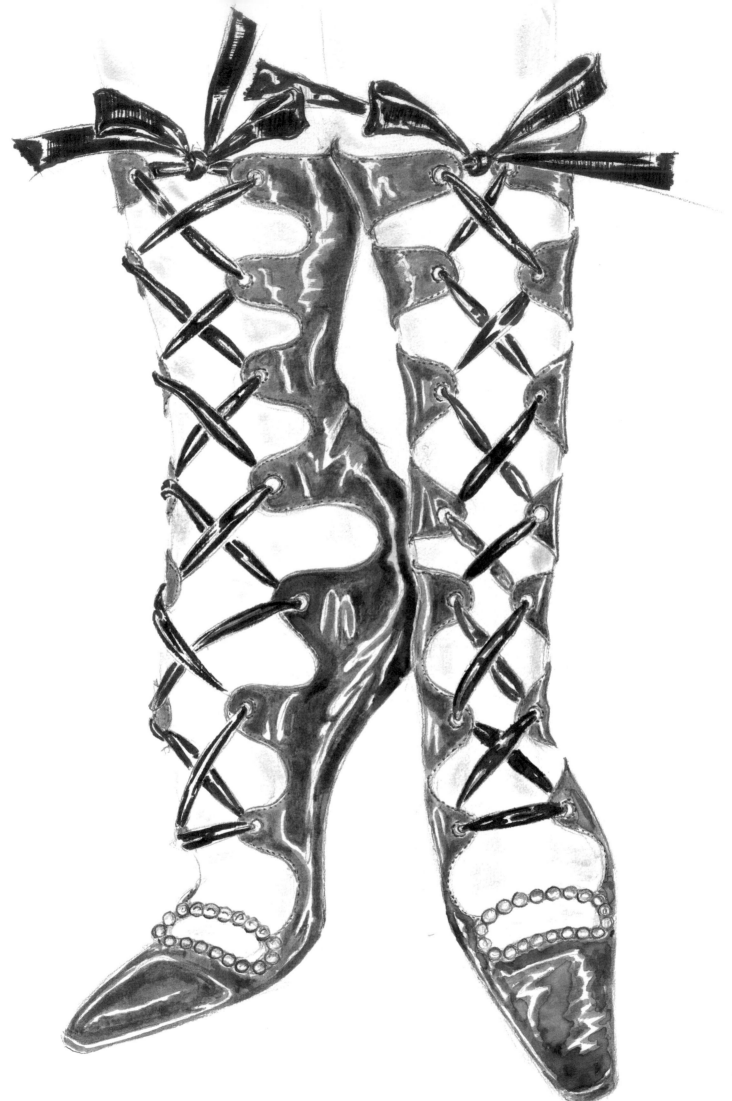

classic

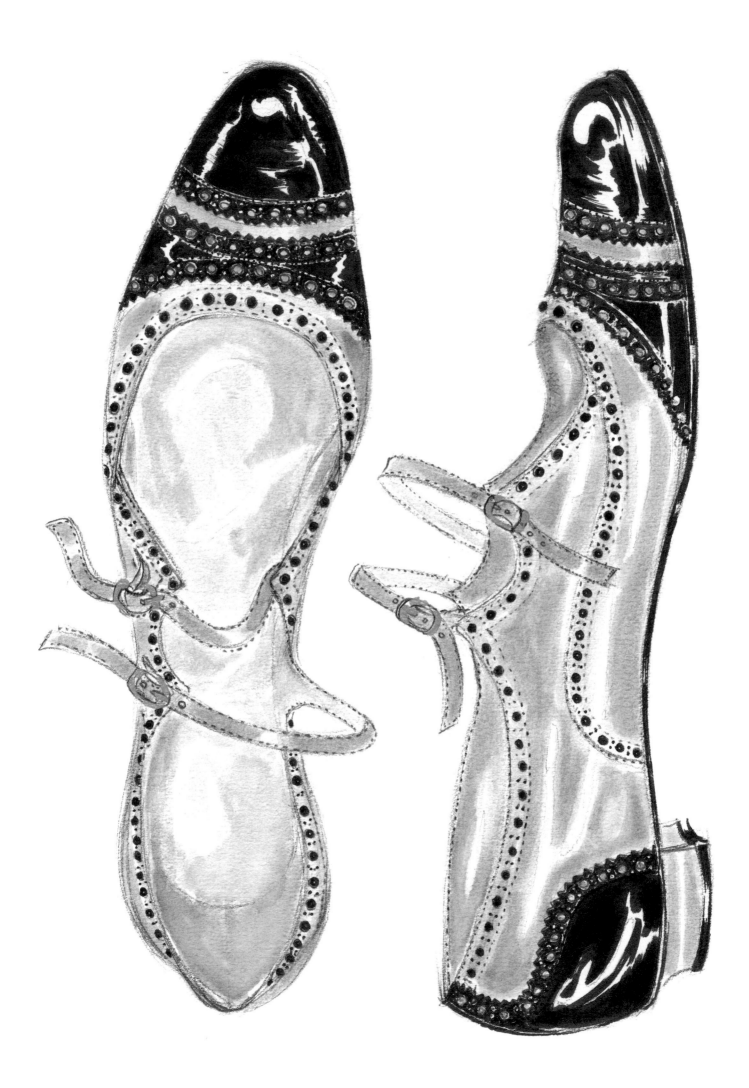

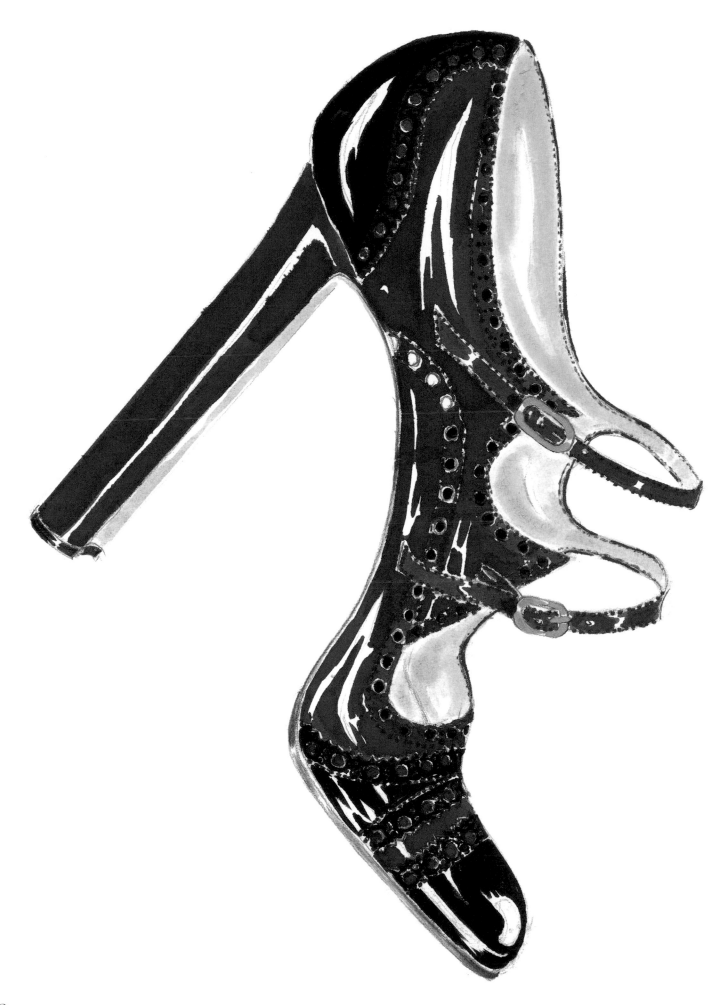

115

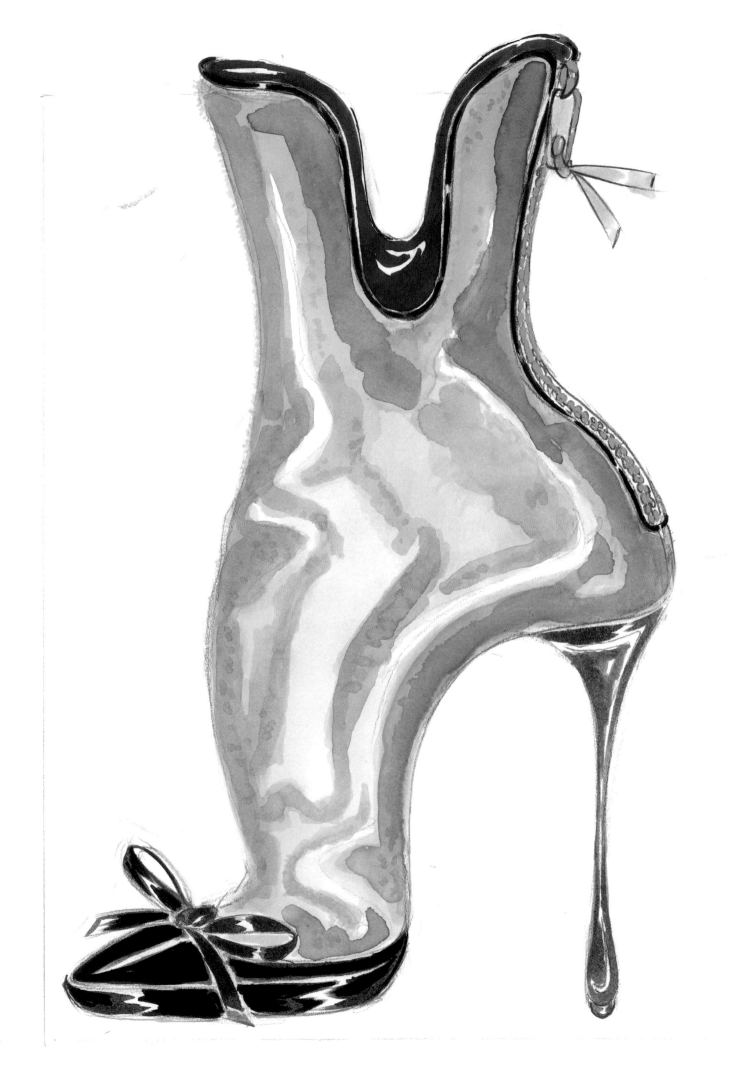

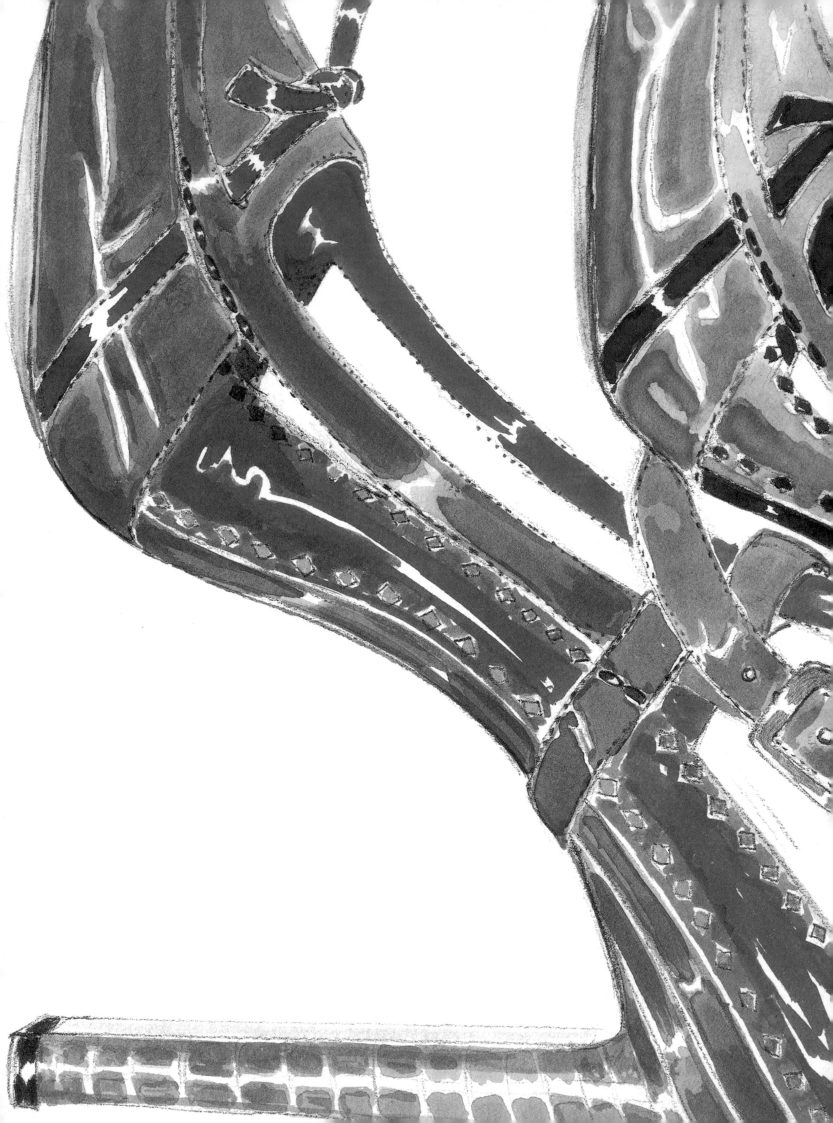

theatrical

I am writing at my desk, shod today in old passementerie-trimmed grey velvet Manolo pumps, with my back supported by a Manolo cushion, a long-ago Christmas gift from the designer. Three steps away is a closet brimming with several hundred pairs of Manolos, dating back a quarter of a century. In the front hall, Manolo's scented candles (also presents from the designer) are burning, and a Manolo notepad, a holiday token of more recent vintage, sits next to the phone. I was married in Manolos, gave birth with a pair of Manolos stashed in the maternity-ward locker, and I expect I'll be buried in Manolos, or maybe the whole extravagant accumulation of them will be buried with me, *à la égyptienne*. I am, in short, a three-decade devotee of the man and his shoes, a habit that has invited, in turns, ridicule (for wearing mules in an era of sneakers), fury (for the money squandered on this passion), and, finally, awe (for possessing possibly the most comprehensive collection of Manolos outside of the master's own archives). Manolo, is it time to name a shoe after me?

Manolo Blahník, his mother said, was born old, but somehow he's managed to preserve his childhood self into his adult life. The first shoes he ever made, as a boy in the Canary Islands, were muslin-and-ribbon slippers for his pet dog, who'd lie on his back and raise his paws while the young master fastened their pink bows – still a signature Manolo embellishment.

Manolo's taste is pitched so high and fine, sometimes words elude him, and he expresses himself by squeals, usually of delight. His ideas are often best conveyed via drawings – Platonic ideals of shoes. A single, allusive sketch of a shoe can suggest a whole narrative of murder, passion, or seduction. Everything Manolo does – dressing, decorating, designing – is filtered through a sensibility so exquisite that the outcome invariably falls on the outer limits of perfection. Or as Manolo would say, 'Beyond!' So full of exuberant life were his rococo creations for the film *Marie Antoinette*, they nearly upstaged the actors. Perpetually animated, Manolo in conversation quivers with excitement; his creations likewise burst with an élan vital. Fringes shimmy, flowers tremble, bows bristle, buckles twinkle.

If Manolo has an Achilles heel, it is his sweet tooth, and so, consequently, the shoes are confectionery – high-glucose bon-bons for the foot. A lover of opera (the more histrionically tortured the diva, the better), Manolo naturally bestows upon his shoes their own peculiar music – the rhythmic staccato of stilettos striking parquet, the dry rattle of pearls swinging from the vamps of mules, the breezy rustle of raffia.

Frequently in pain – his back chronically aches him – Manolo wouldn't dream of inflicting such an unpleasant sensation on a woman. The shoes are engineered anatomically, taking into account the filigree bones, delicate muscles, and fragile sinews of the foot. Manolo understands intimately their placement, their patterns, their movements.

His tapering, graceful silhouettes attenuate an instep, slim an ankle, elongate a calf, refine the full head-to-toe line of a woman's physique. They buoy up the whole woman to the point of levitation, lifting her in body and spirit. Innately courtly and decent, Manolo cannot make vulgar, coarse, or clumsy shoes. Not for him are feet of clay.

A polyglot, Manolo speaks six languages fluently and sometimes simultaneously. His references ricochet alarmingly from Paulina Borghese to Tina Chow, from Fellini to Sandra Dee, from Taormina to tweeds, Byzantium to botany. Animal, vegetable and mineral; history and culture; nature and artifice – all are compressed into every design. A girl in Manolos becomes a universal heroine.

A hothouse hybrid – he is all at once Czech, Spanish, African, and British – Manolo conjures up chimeras. His drawings, like those in a medieval bestiary, are bizarre, exotic, perverse, and emblematic – gorgeous mutations born of a cross-pollinated imagination.

Manolo is forever faithful to himself – even his sleek, symmetrical manner of brushing back his hair is unchanging – and so his design aesthetic is constant. He resists, for example, platforms or inordinate toe cleavage. Though he may have formulated today's wide-ranging shoe taxonomy – from Mary Janes to gladiators – he knows intuitively just how far to go too far. A perfect foot – arch high, second toe longer than the first – was created first by God, and then by Praxiteles. But the perfect shoe is always by Manolo.

AMY FINE COLLINS
Special Correspondent to *Vanity Fair*

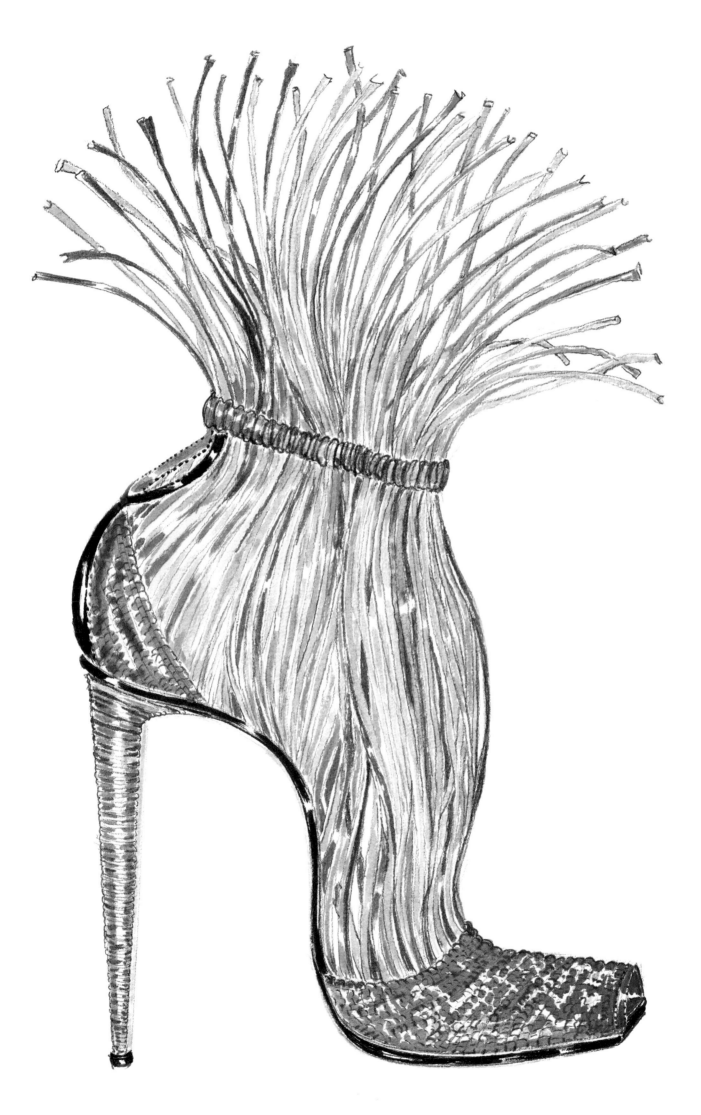

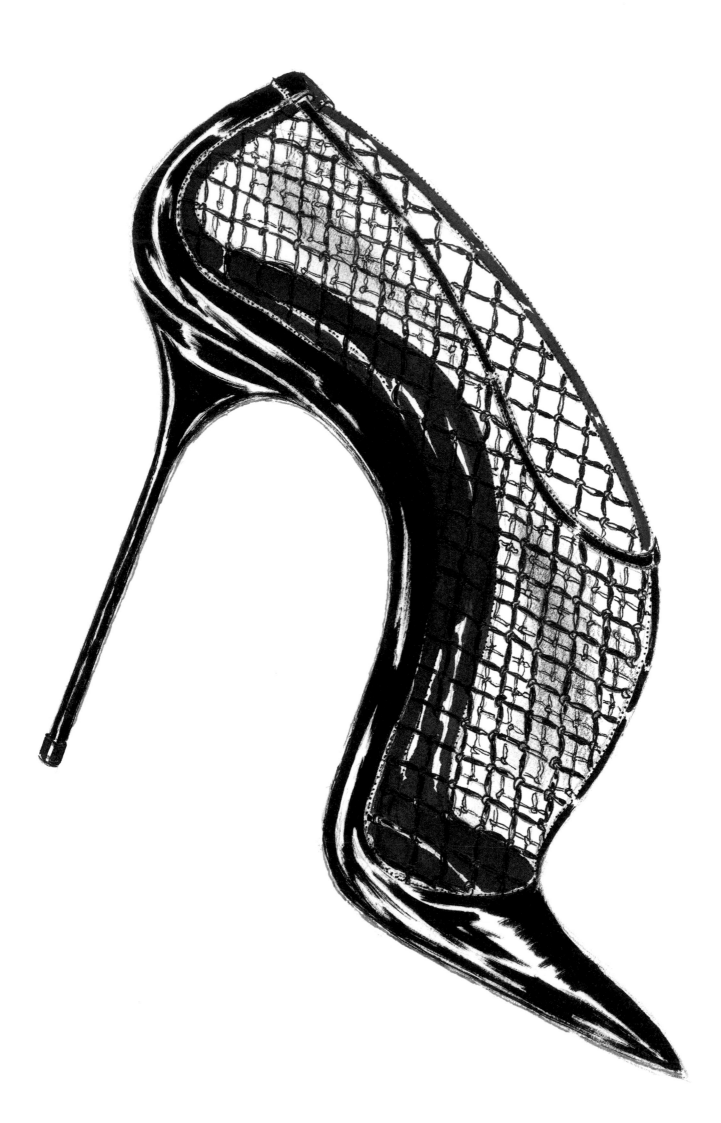

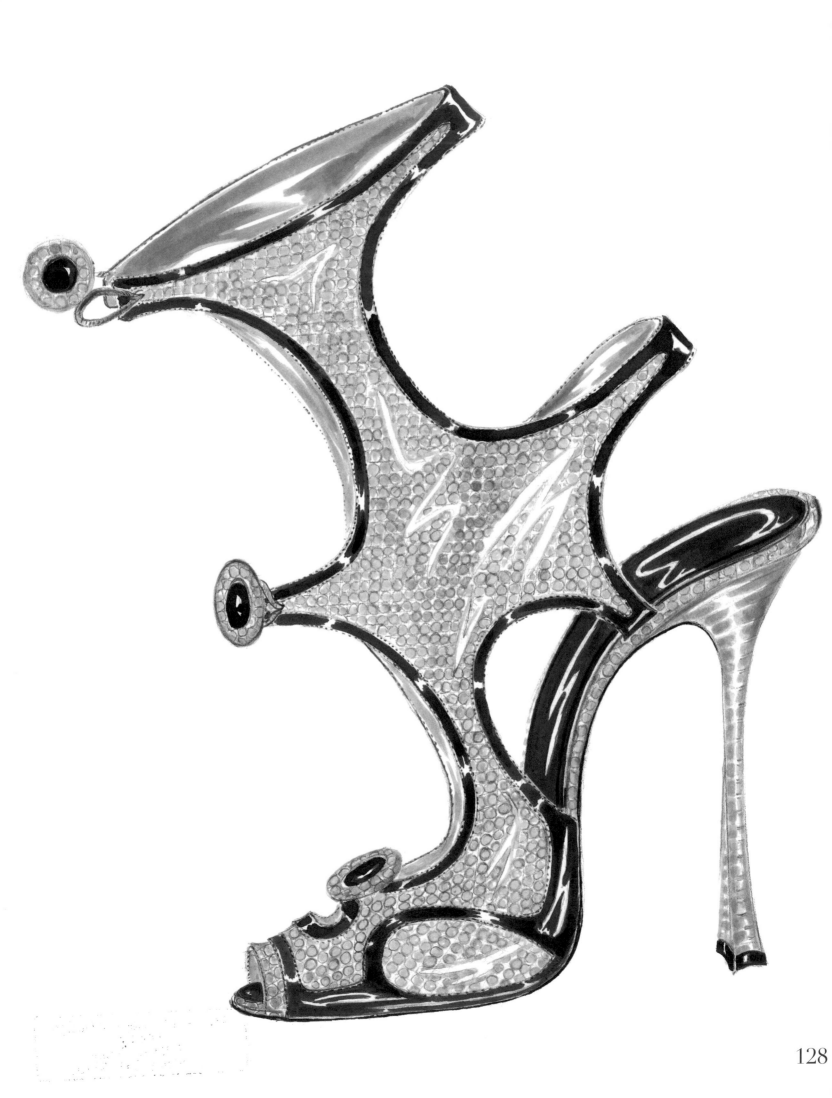

128

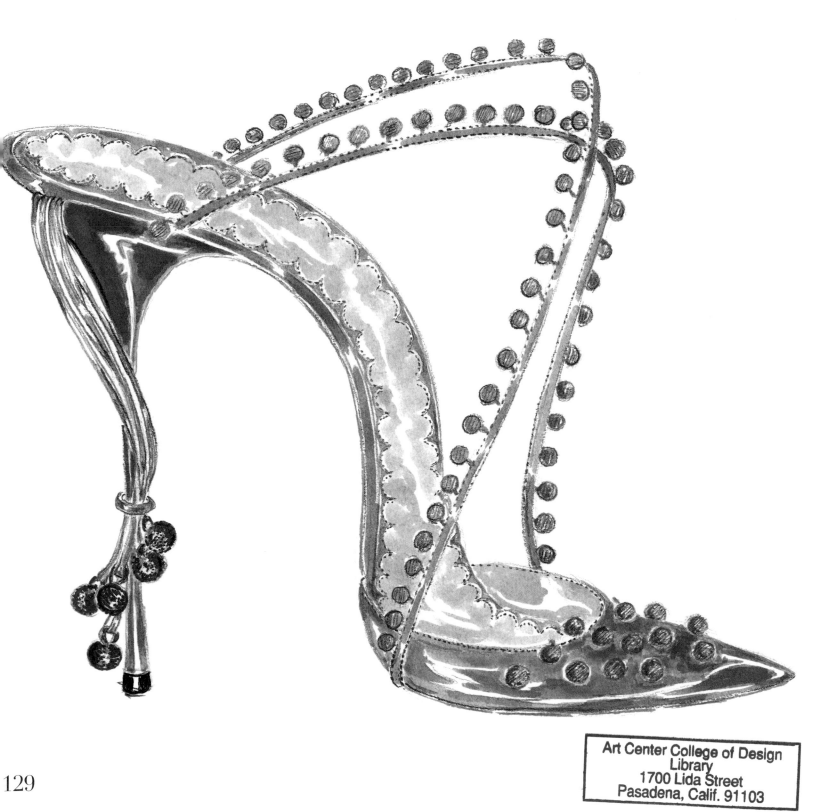

129

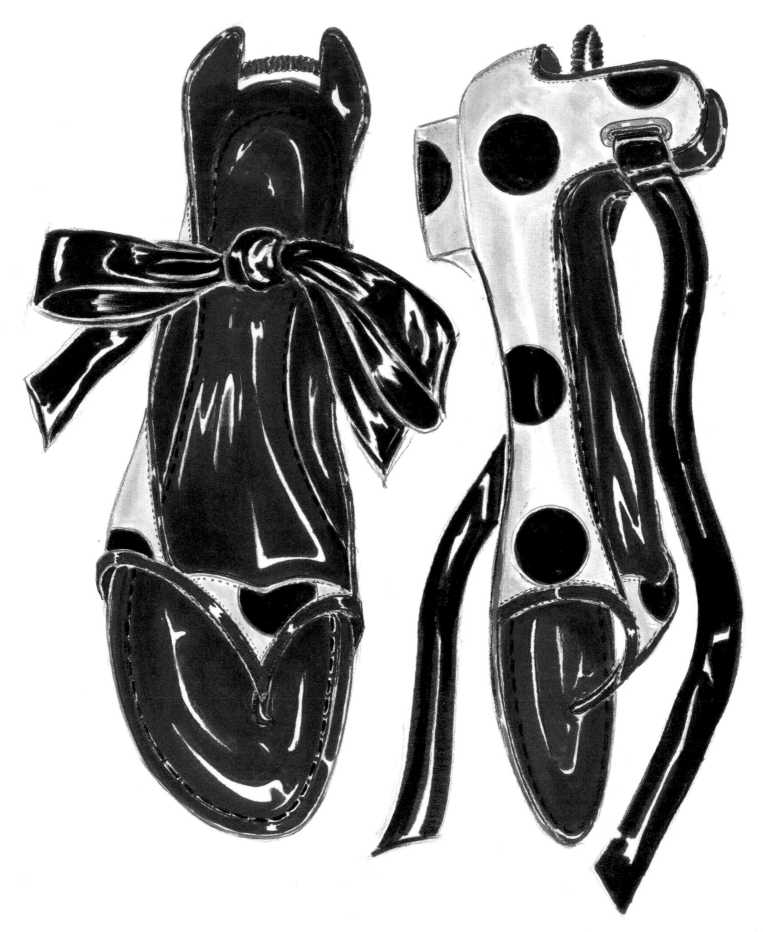

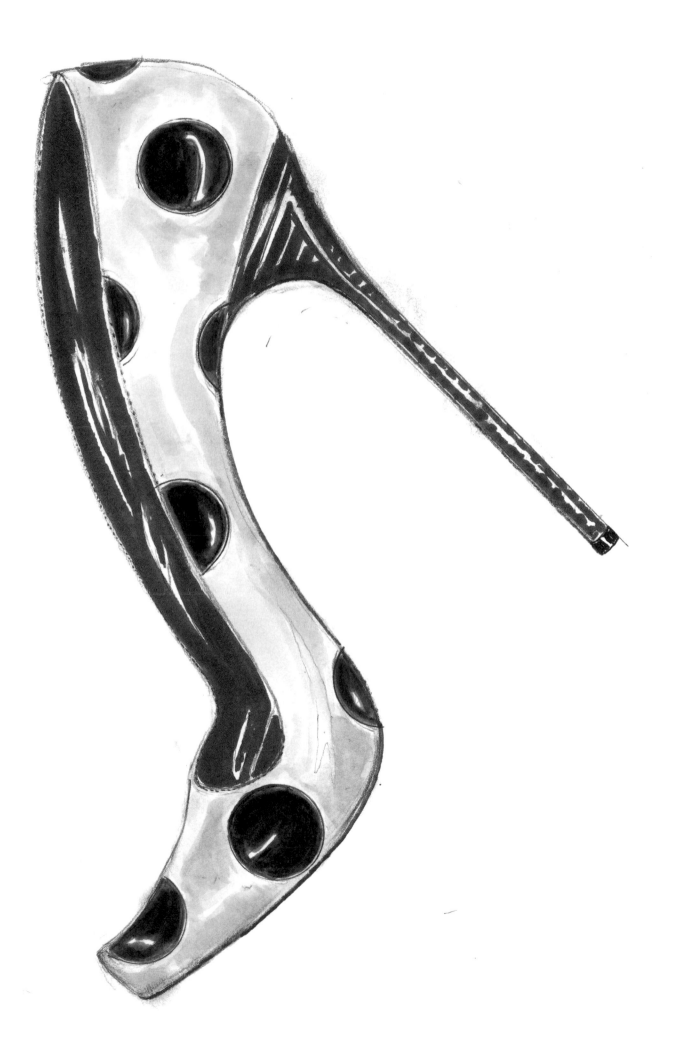

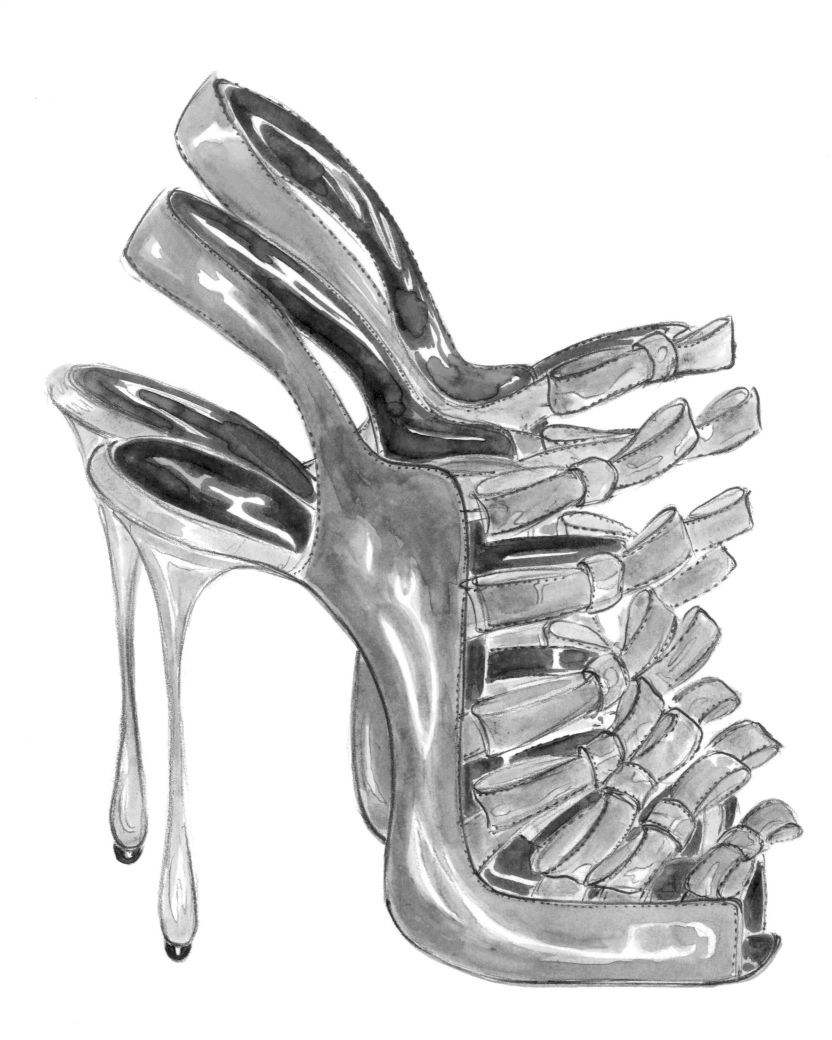

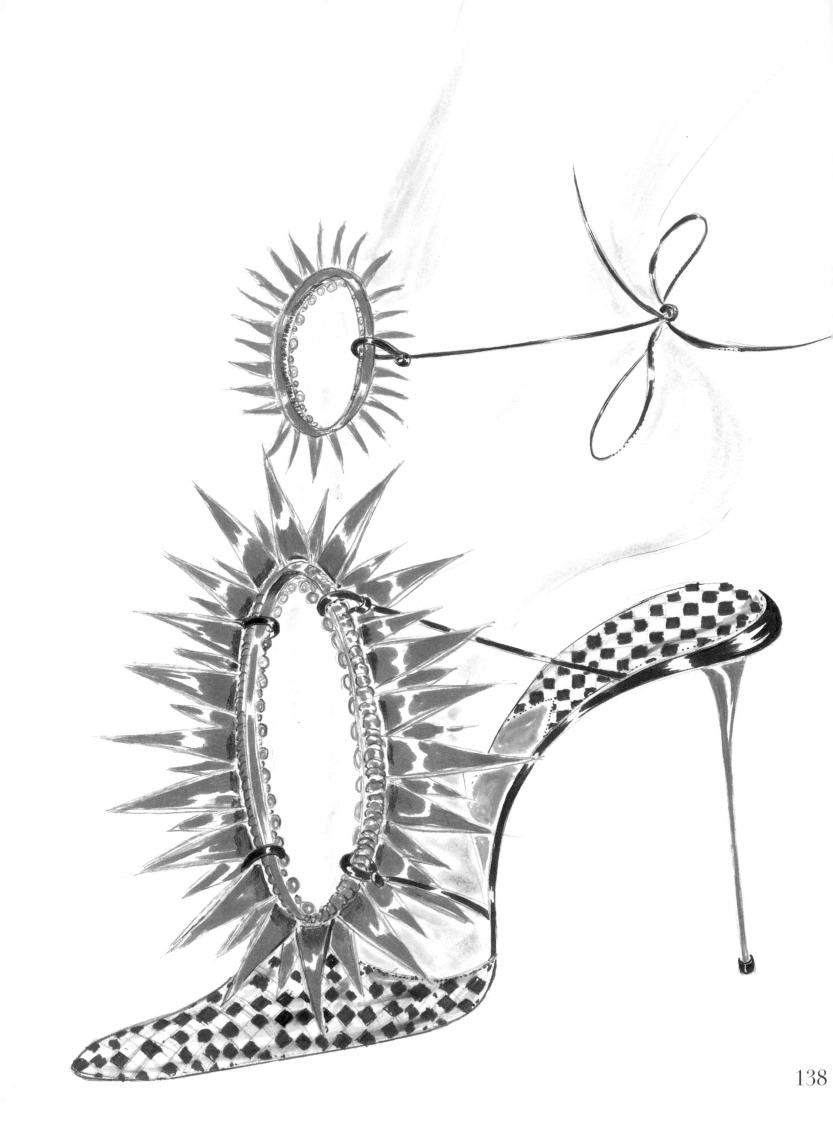

rome and greece

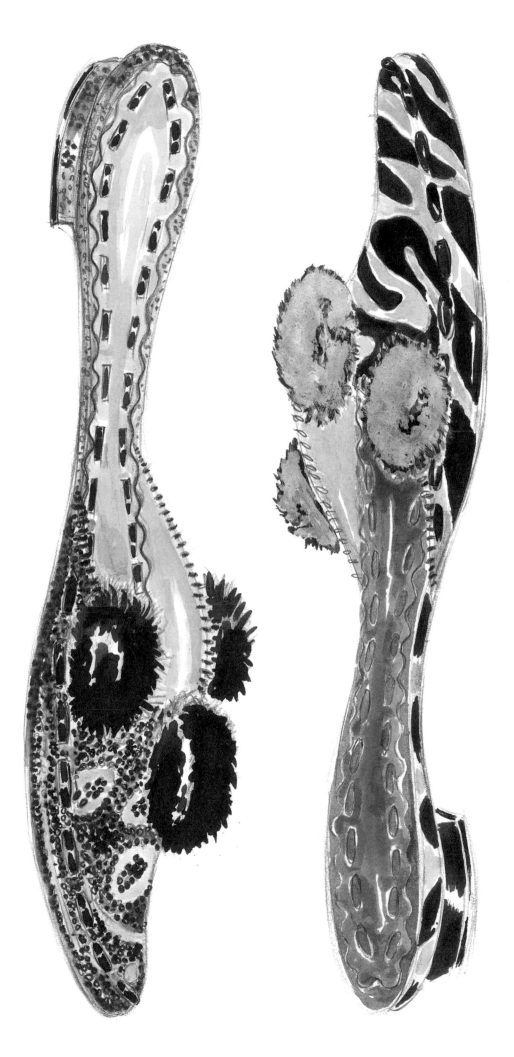

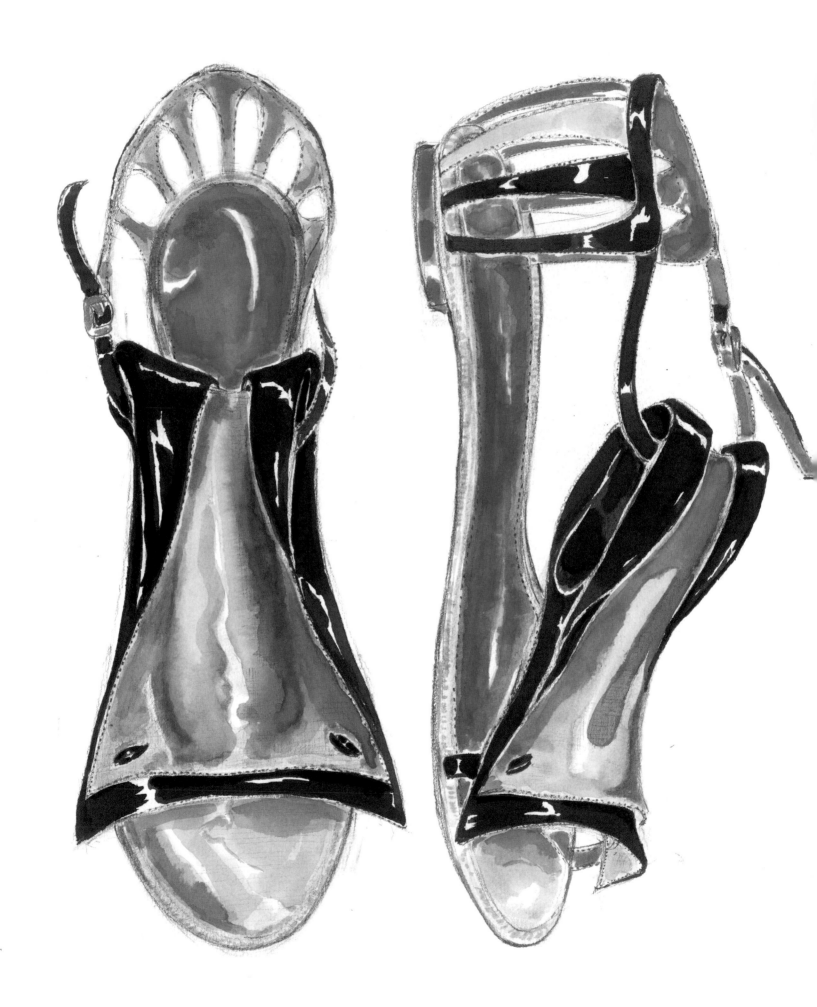

145

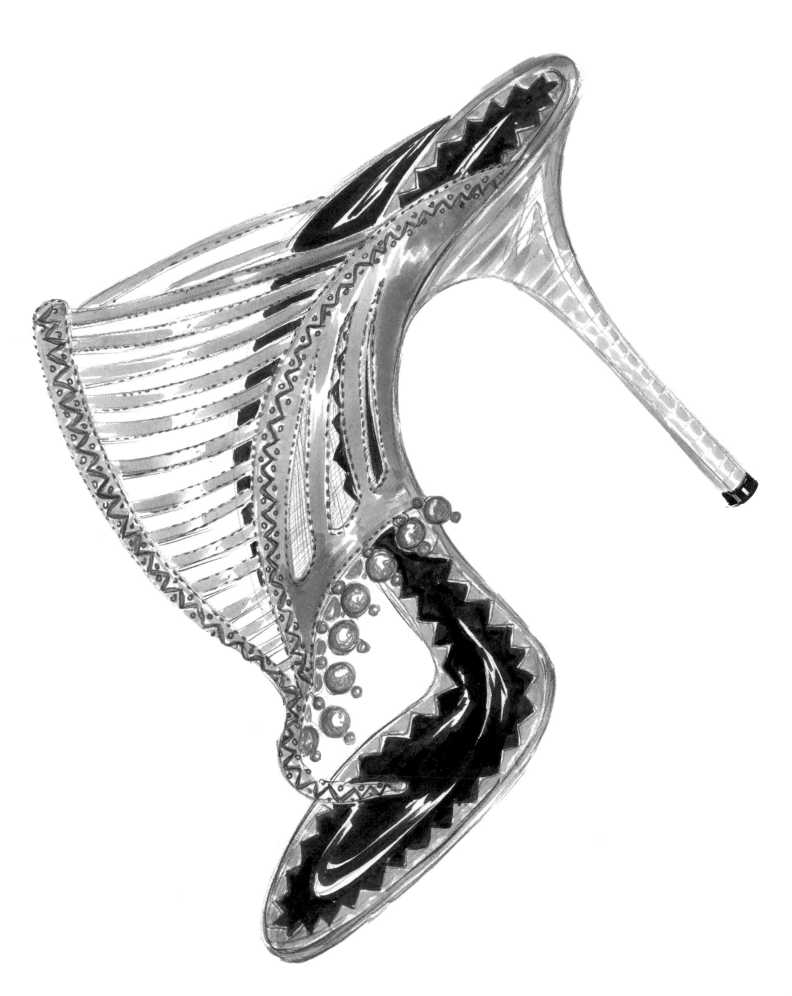

'I opened the window at six and stepped out on the broad terrace in front. I looked over an almost level expanse of green that ended in crevasses which seemed to plunge like glaciers into blueness. I knew this must be the Mediterranean, but could not see the surface, nor have I all day, for sea and sky are not to be distinguished from each other. But the sea makes itself felt by its smell of salt and iodine, and its endless lament comes up from the foot of the precipices. A little later I seemed to see a high, level mountain range capped with snow. It was an effect of the sea and cloud seen in perspective.

'We went out at ten and found Caputo, the superintendent, at the ruins, with a handsome and attractive young man, the architect named Carbonara. He turned out as delightful in mind as he is in body. With him in fore- and afternoon we took a general look at the ancient town. It is of immense extent and beauty of ruins and landscape will hound me all my life.

'But the great spring gushing out of a cave, and the sites of the sanctuaries, of the agoras, and of the temples of Zeus are very impressive. Of statuary we have as yet seen but a single important one. A seated Demeter, a copy (unfortunately a poor one) of a marvellous original, a *Mater Dolorosa*, a rather rare thing in fifth-century Greek art. The air was very sparkling and vivifying, but cold. Toward sunset I should have perished but for the blessed fur lining.'

Bernard Berenson, Cyrene, 16 April 1935, as quoted in Roloff Beny, *The Thrones of Earth and Heaven*, 1958

russia

154

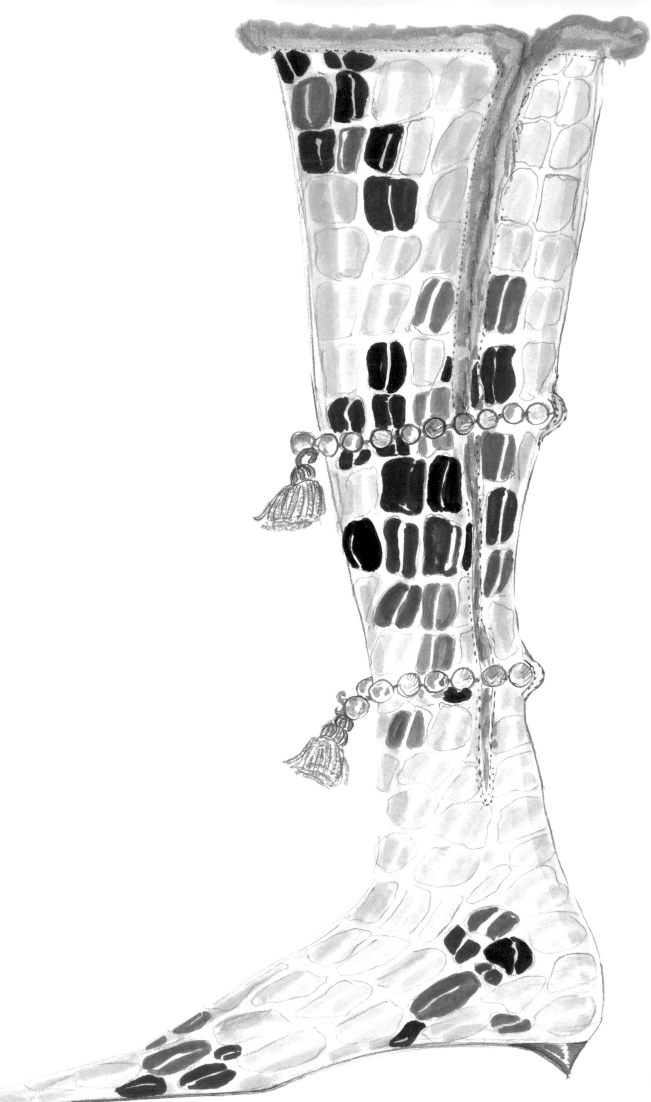

'As for clothes, I resolved to have two suits, one for every day and one for best. When once I had got them I felt sure I should wear them a long time. I purposely trained myself to wear a suit for two and a half years, and in fact I discovered a secret: for clothes always to look new and not to get shabby they should be brushed as often as possible, five or six times a day. Brushing does not hurt the cloth. I speak from knowledge. What does hurt it is dust and dirt. Dust is the same thing as stones if you look at it through the microscope, and, however hard a brush is, it is almost the same as fur. I trained myself to wear my boots evenly. The secret lies in putting down the whole sole at once, and avoiding treading on the side. One can train oneself to this in a fortnight, after that the habit is unconscious. In this way boots last on an average a third as long again. That is the experience of two years.'

Fyodor Dostoevsky, *The Adolescent*, 1875

urban

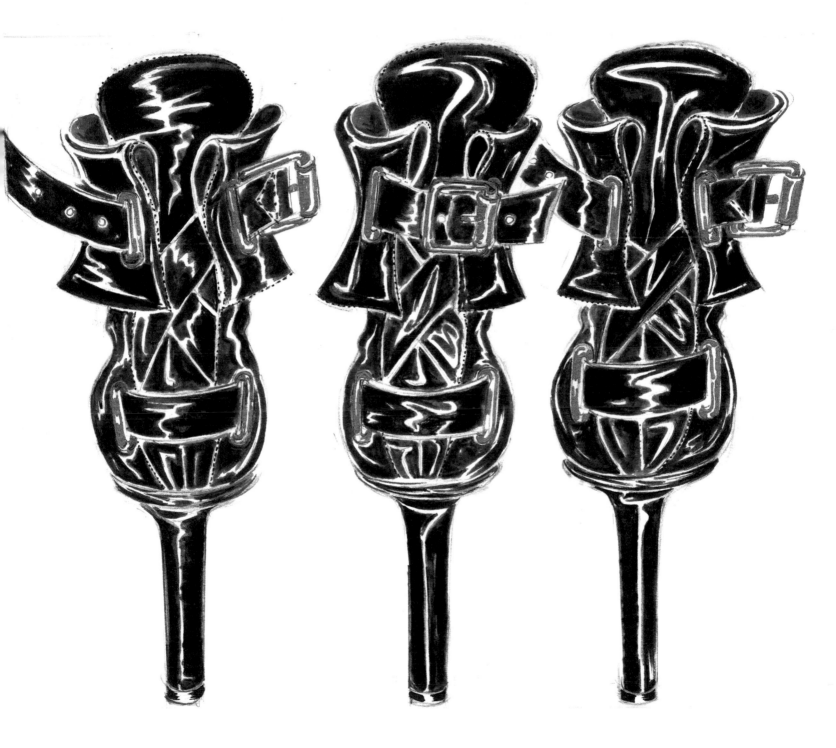

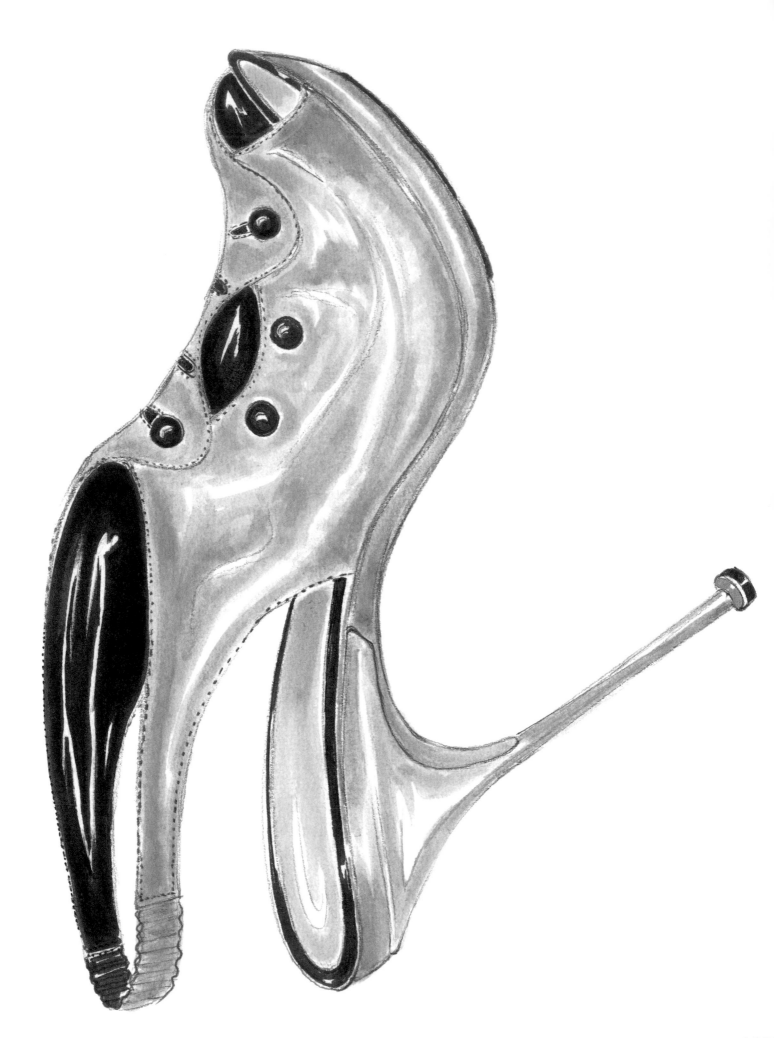

162

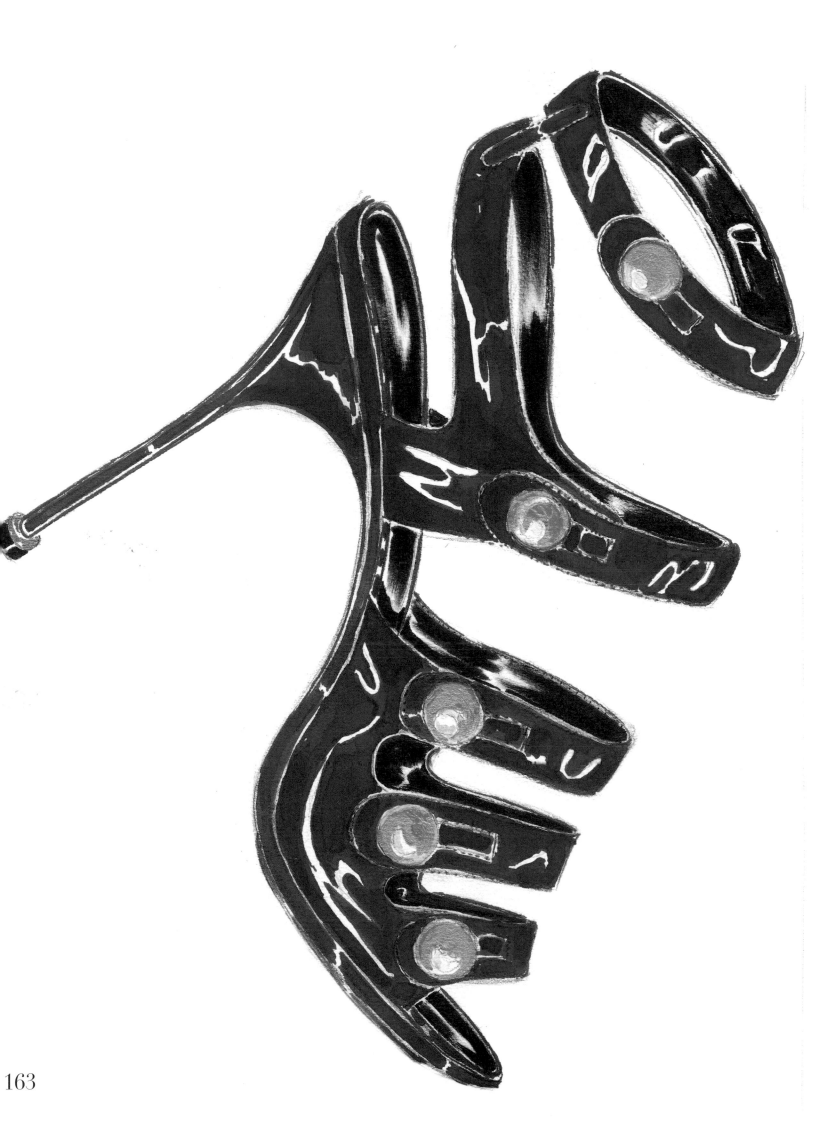

163

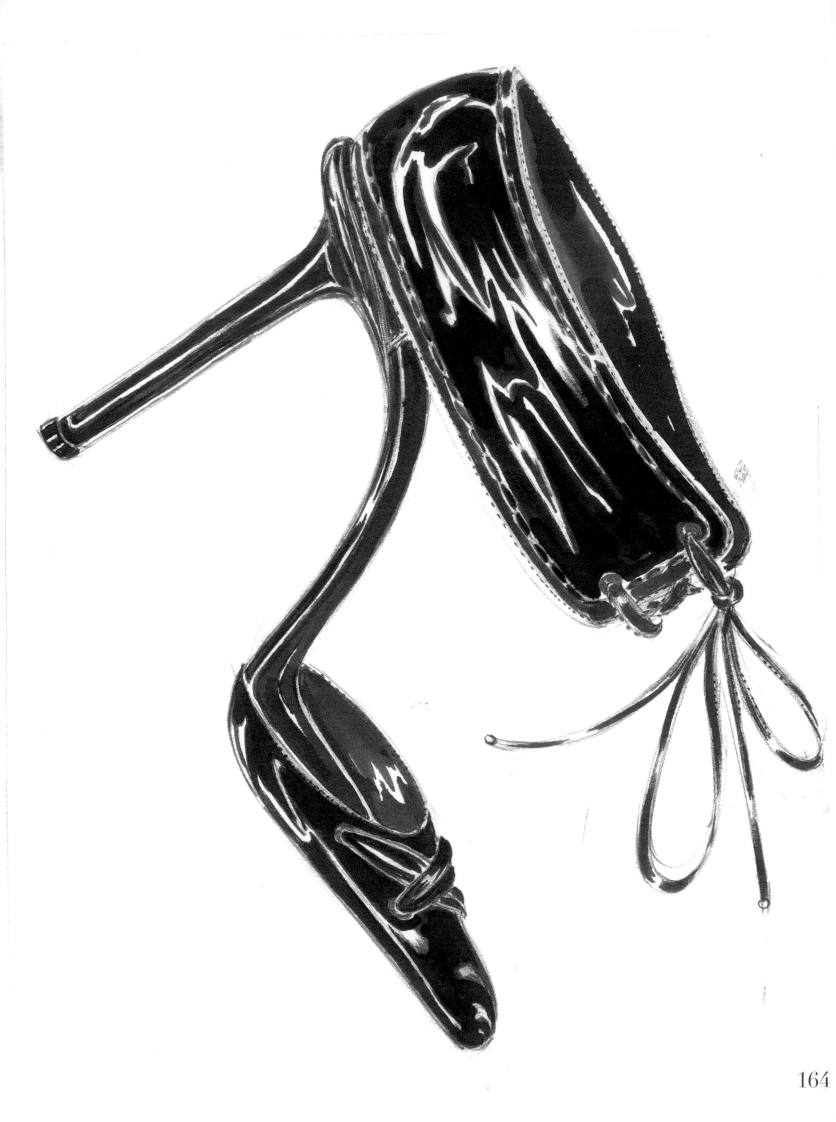

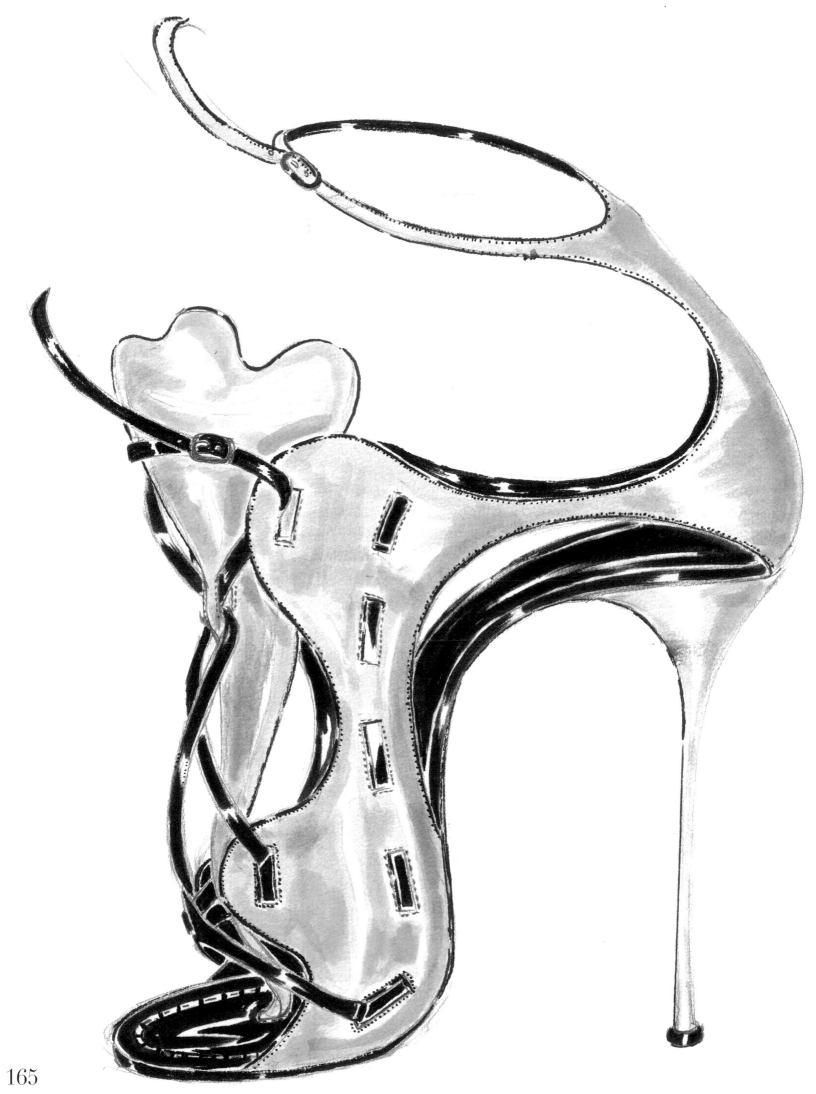

165

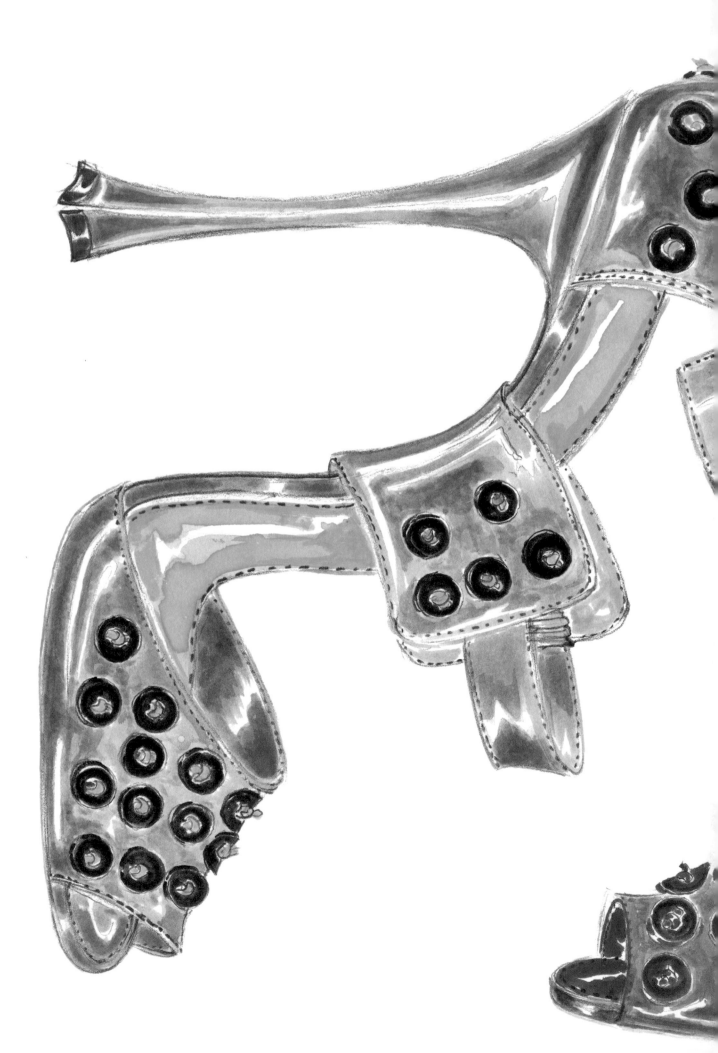

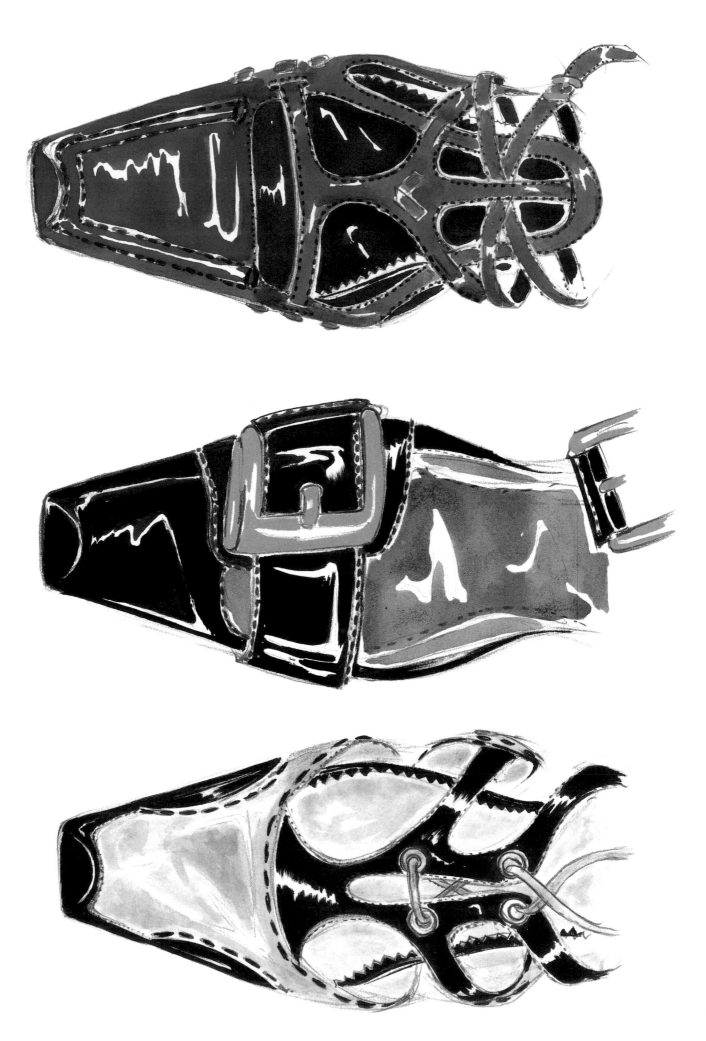

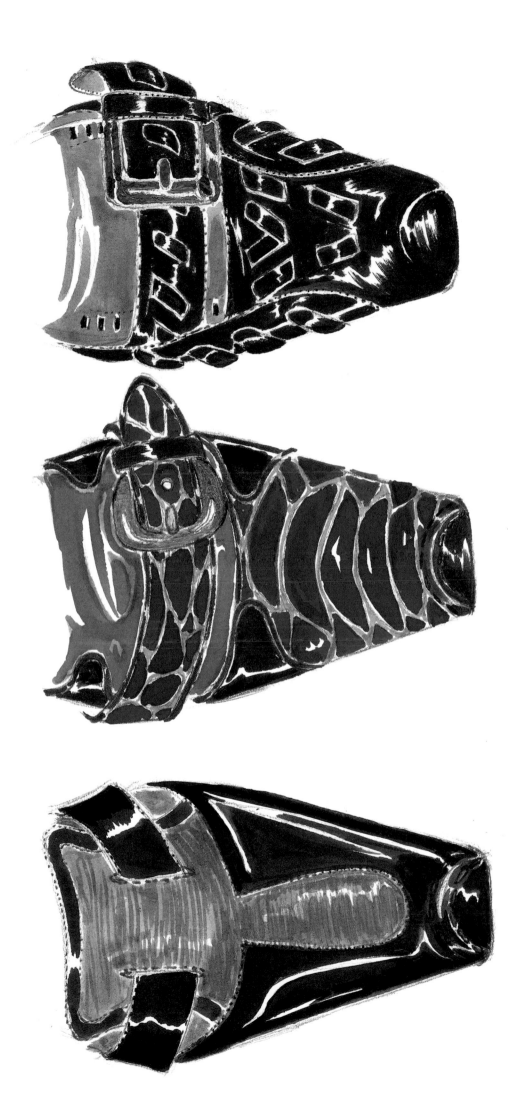

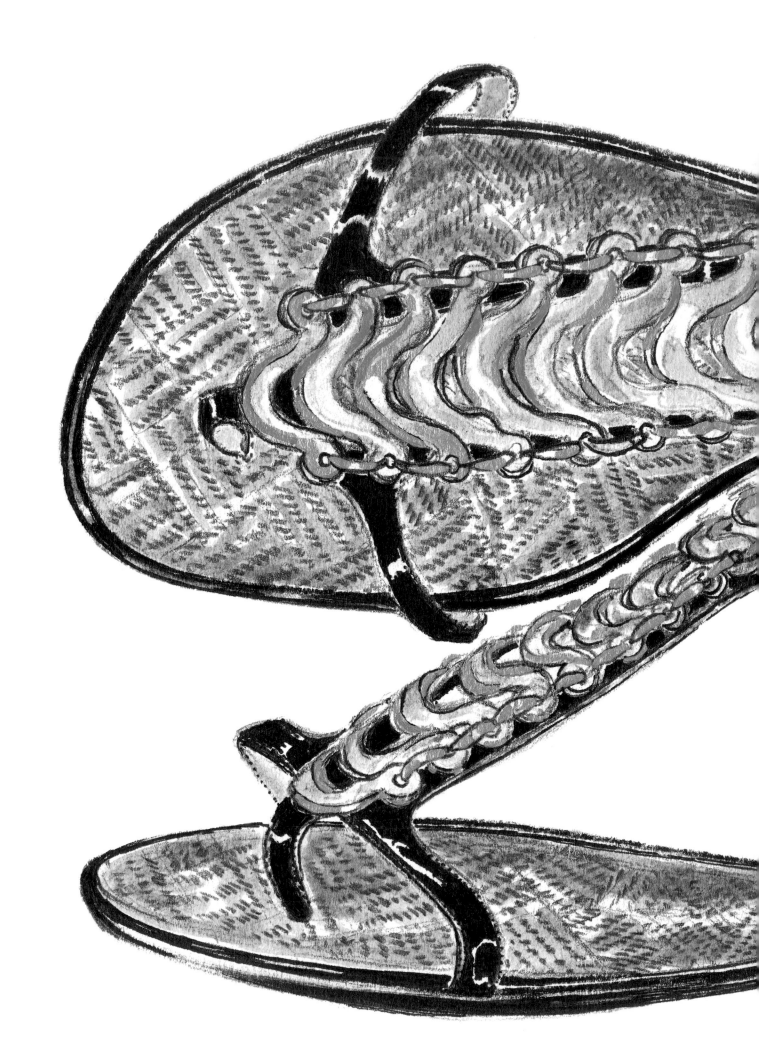

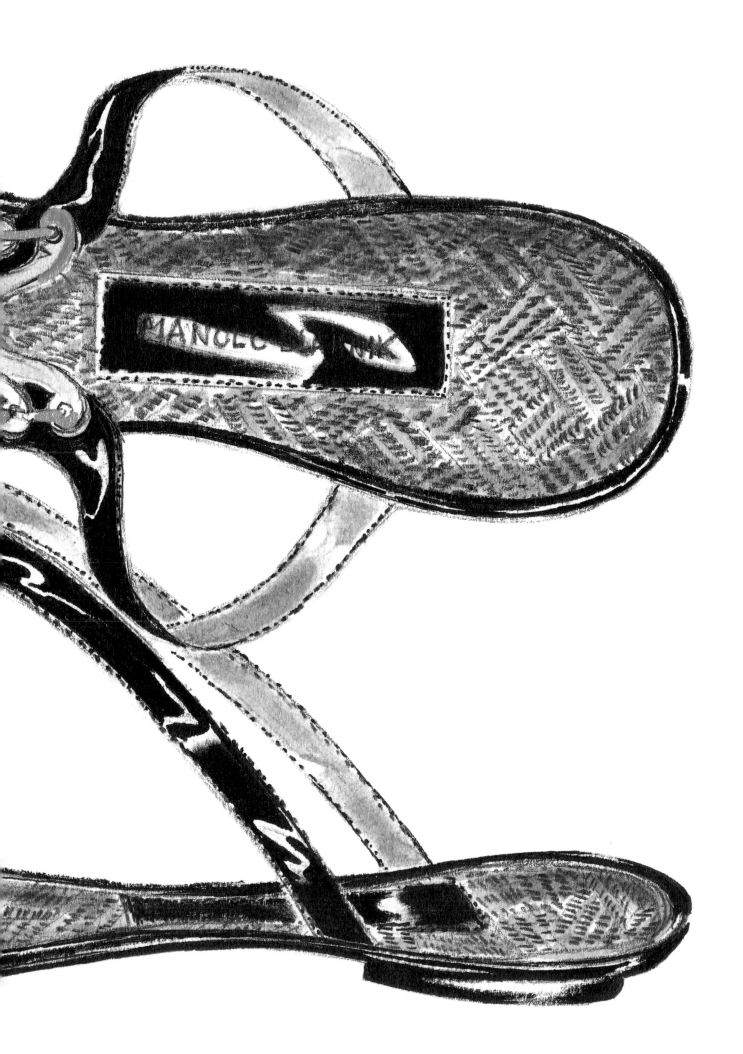

modernist

174

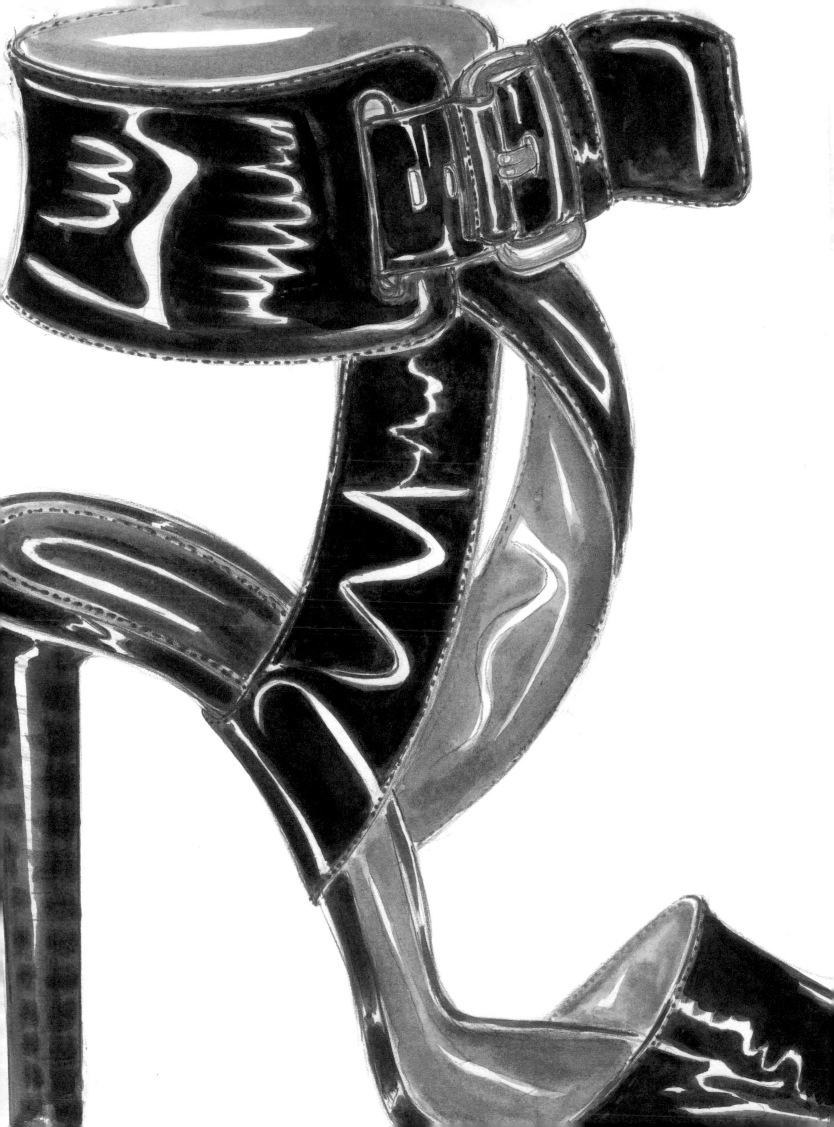

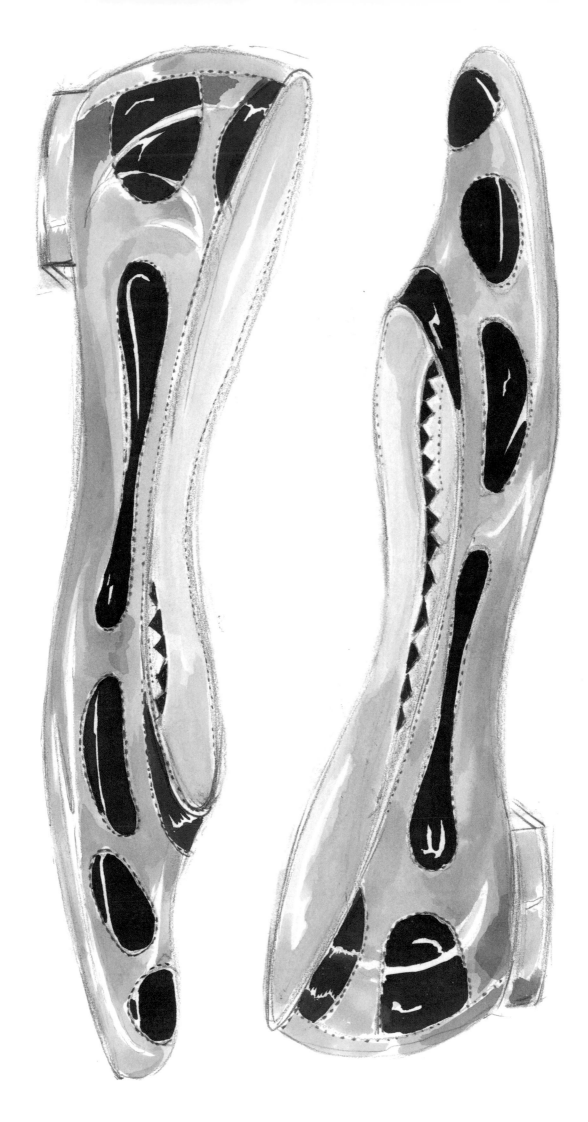

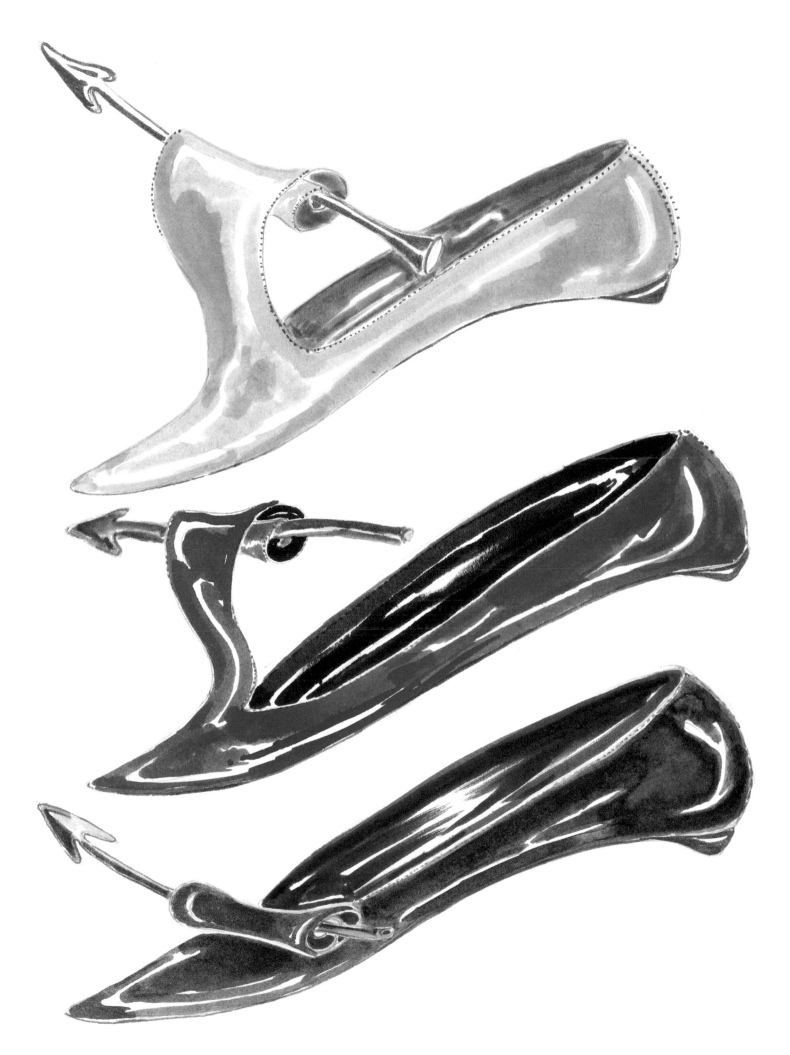

christmas

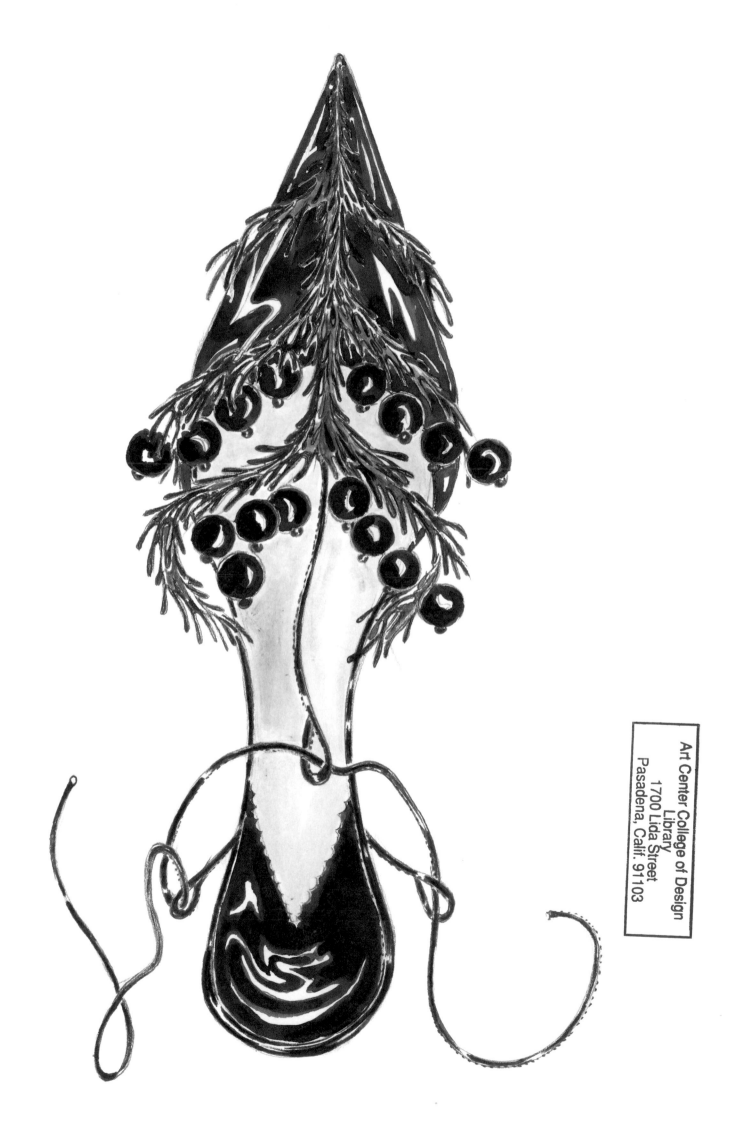

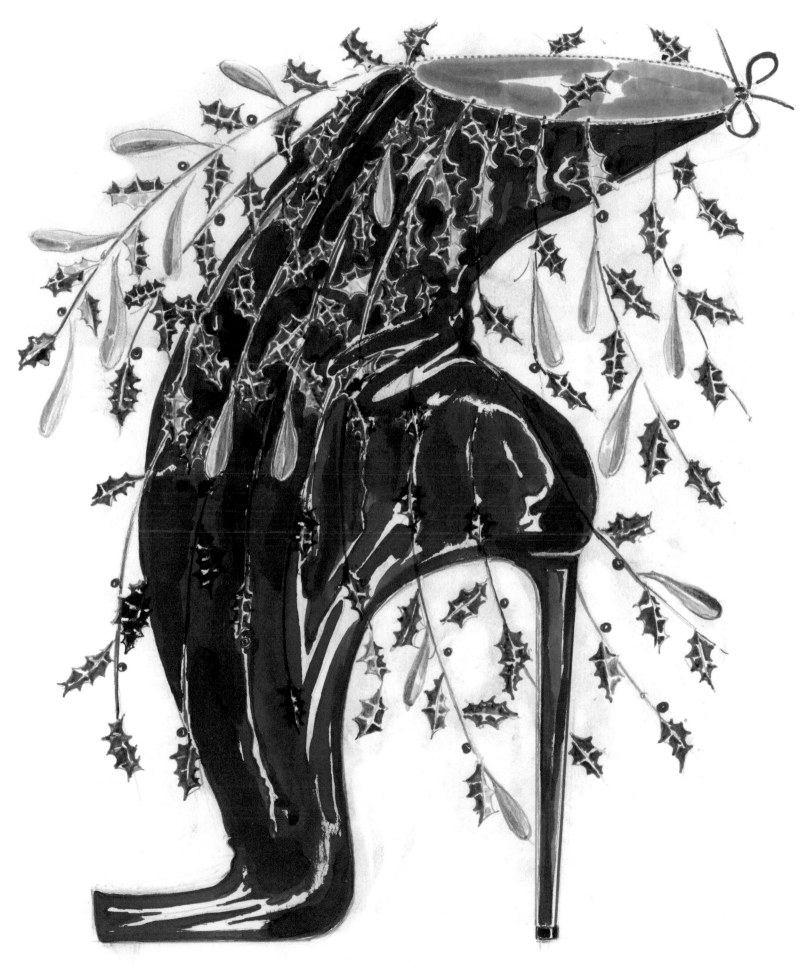

189

My Christmas Box ^{SHOE} hanging on
a nail. Manolo Blahnik
Happy times 2.... — "Vogue" Spain

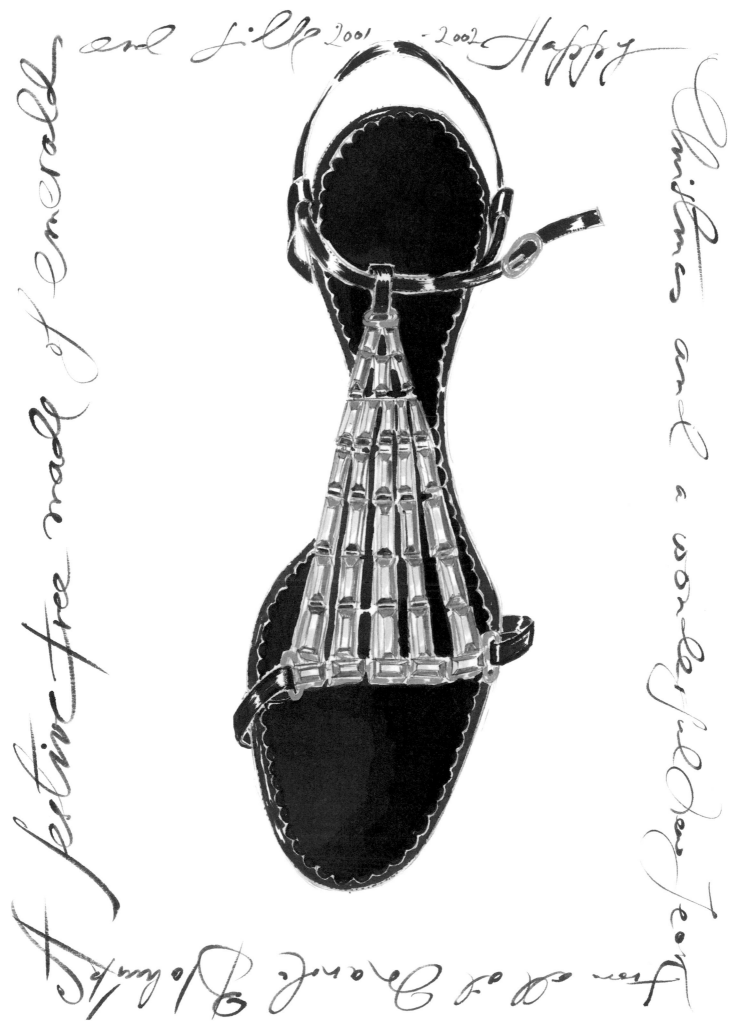

Happy Christmas and a wonderful New Year to all of Manolo Blahnik's festive friends and Jilly 2001 - 2002 and love of emerald

191

captions

37 *Sagan* (AW04/05). Layered thigh-high boot, in suede, with stitched suede circles and suede loops lined in leather, hooked together with suede-covered buttons, on a 'Seno' heel.

39 *Féria de Sevilla* (2001). Silk evening mule, with Spanish pom-pom decoration, bells and leather ties.

40–41 *Carmencita* (2002). Satin evening shoe, with silk Spanish fringe on velvet Mokuba ribbon, and Spanish pom-pom decoration.

42 *Estrellita* (2008). Satin sandal, with silk fringe and silk pom-poms; for *Vogue España*, 20th anniversary issue.

43 *Lola* (2003). Leather *redecilla* (trellis) bottine, with Spanish silk pom-poms; a homage to Doña Lola Flores; for *Vogue España*, 15th anniversary issue.

45 *Paget* (SS00). Heel-less satin evening shoe, with knotted silk-thread tassles.

47 *Sarola* (AW08/09). Cantilevered leather bottine, with side lacing.

48 *Kandos* (AW07/08). Patent leather open-toed bottine, with back lacing, on a teardrop heel.

49 *Delis* (AW08/09). Open-toed nappa shoe boot, with satin trim.

50 *Ballet Extrême* (2005). Satin 'ballerina' bottine, with removable lycra sock; a homage to the ballerina Moira Shearer.

51 *Ballet* (2005). Satin bottine, with removable lycra sock.

52 *Patra* (AW07/08). Pony shoe, trimmed in leather, on a teardrop heel.

53 *Pirea* (AW07/08). Lace-up leather shoe with cut-out detail and contrast lining, on a teardrop heel.

54 *Esparta* (SS07). Flat calfskin sandal, with leather detail and hand-painted edges, lined in vivid violet.

55 *Innamor* (AW09/10). Gold leather evening sandal, with chocolate brown silk-satin 'pelmet' cut to almost touch the floor, on a gilded heel.

56–57 *Cortesana* (2005). Red doeskin chopine, on an elevated cork base covered in nappa.

58–59 *Rebord* (SS10). Tiered-front sandal, inspired by the New York Guggenheim Museum structure by Frank Lloyd Wright, in vitello grasso.

60 *Disso* (AW10/11). Bottine in vitello grasso, buttoned under the sole.

61 *Trikoupis* (AW10/11). Leather walking shoe, with contrasting gold trim, and spotted silk lining, on a 'Brancusian' heel. Based on the Parthenon figures.

63 *Anelli* (SS97). Patent leather shoe, with circular cut-outs, on a perforated resin heel.

64 *Aksham* (SS08). Suede shoe with ankle detail in contrasting cut-outs and leather trim, inspired by windows of Turkish houses overlooking the Bosphorus, on a 'Clavo' ('nail') heel.

65 *Dos* (SS10). Suede sandal, with padded circular accessories and contrasting leather lining.

66 *Titanium* (SS03). Sandal on lightweight aluminium base, with leather straps to thread through the holes, on an angular heel.

67 *Tufa* (SS09). Hand-knotted nappa sandal.

68 *Tilda* (2006). Open-toed Scottish ghillie, with steel heel-less base and bronze rings. Exhibited in the 'blog.mode: addressing fashion' exhibition at the Metropolitan Museum of Art, New York.

69 *Screw* (2004). Leather day shoe, with titanium base, and a screwed-on curved heel in titanium.

70–71 *Arunium* (SS05). Heel-less sandal, with titanium body, covered in brown embossed leather, with bronze decoration inspired by medieval nails; for Jean-Paul Gaultier Couture.

72 *Tunisia* (SS04). Two-tone leather sandal, on a stacked leather heel.

73 *Erdem* (SS07). Day shoe with triangular cut-outs in leather, with contrasting lining.

75 *Ebete* (SS10). Open-toed, slit bottine, with side lacing and contrasting lining in satin or leather with painted edges.

76 *Horlia* (2007). Articulated sandal in hand-stitched hide, with leather ties and metal buckles.

77 *Male* (2008). Articulated two-tone sandal in satin with contrasting leather lining.

78 *Espeso* (SS07). Leather, open-toed mule with leather straps, on a hand-painted wooden stacked heel.

79 *Bu* (SS08). Side lacing, open-toed slingback, with metal eyelets and contrasting lining, on a 'Clavo' ('nail') heel in striped pony.

80 *Fano* (AW08/09). Samurai boot, with metal buckles, on a painted stacked wooden heel.

81 *Breda* (SS07). Black patent open-toed shoe, with metal eyelets, on a hand-painted stacked wooden heel.

82 *Tisica* (AW03/04). Nappa mule with metal rings on hand-stitched loops.

83 *Bou* (SS08). Articulated sandal on an elevated 'spoon' sole and a 'Clavo' ('nail') heel.

84 *Bossa* (SS04). Leather sandal with ankle straps and bronze rings and rivets.

85 *Shiku* (AW02/03). Knee-length boot in Moss Rose pony, with belt detail and covered buttons, lined in vivid orange.

87 *Bali* (2005). Satin evening shoe, with green and aqua painted coral trim, on a white coral heel, reinforced with steel.

88 *Momella* (SS08). Dancing shoe, with bullion-embroidered cherries, and tiered, degrade dyed marabou feathers on green satin, on a 'Clavo' ('nail') heel.

89 *Princesa de Asturias* (2004). Satin court shoe, hand-embroidered with lily of the valley motif and silk flowers.

90 *Patoso* (AW08/09). Pewter leather bottine, hand-embroidered with metal disks, and sea shells, inspired by medieval armour.

91   *Principe de Lampedusa* (2003). Red satin evening shoe with antique Sicilian coral entwined in strips of gold nappa.

93   *Isabella* (2005). Botanical sandal with agave leaf motif, in suede, decorated with acorns.

94   *Toubid* (SS09). Suede and leather sandal, inspired by sea anemone 'blanda', on a leather-covered heel.

95   *Ginkgo* (SS08). Satin evening shoe, with silk ginkgo biloba leaves, on a 'twisted' resin heel.

96   *The Olive* (2002). Satin evening shoe, with silk olive-leaf ties, resin 'olives', on a 'cocktail stick' heel.

97   *Calla lily* (2002). Nappa mule on a titanium Calla lily base.

100–101 From left to right: *Lamour* (AW06/07). Silk-satin court shoe with ruched front using 18th-century ruching technique.
Ataram (AW06/07). Silk-satin court shoe with silk rosette and crystal brooch, based on a door handle from Marie Antoinette's boudoir.
Pupella (AW06/07). Ottoman silk-satin court shoe with draped front.
Sifena (AW06/07). Silk-velvet court shoe, inset with crystal brooches.

102 *Versailles* (2005). Pink silk court shoe, with hand-frayed silk bows and rosettes with glass-bead trim; for Sofia Coppola's *Marie Antoinette*, with costume designer Milena Canonero.

103 *Trianon* (2005). Silk-taffeta mule, with hand-frayed silk bow and rosettes and grosgrain braid; for Sofia Coppola's *Marie Antoinette*, with costume designer Milena Canonero.

104 From top to bottom: *Imperia* (AW06/07). Spotted silk-velvet court shoe, with Czech garnet accessory, and ruby pendant.
Stanisla (AW06/07). Midnight blue satin shoe, with crystal buckle accessory.
Solongio (AW06/07). Royal blue satin shoe-boot, with gold and jet buckle.

105 *Rosaurof* (AW05/06). Shoe in Etro paisley, lined and trimmed in chinchilla, fastened with velvet ribbon.

106 *Caryathis* (AW04/05). Crêpe de Chine boot, with silk bows and pearl buckle inset.

107 *Lady Hamilton* (2006). Yellow satin mule, with hand-frayed edges, tourmaline buckle and striped ottoman silk lining; limited edition for *British Vogue*, 90th anniversary issue.

109 *Pagana* (SS09). Pink and white leather spectator shoe, on a hand-painted wooden heel.

110 *Urfa* (SS08). Black-and-white bulgaro sandal, lined in spotted linen by Canepa, on a hand-stitched opanca-technique base.

111 *Olfa* (AW04/05). Leather and Scottish tweed shoe.

112 *Astruk* (SS08). Flat two-tone spectator Mary Jane in kidskin.

113 *Atrukalta* (SS08). High-heeled two-toned spectator Mary Jane in kidskin.

114 *Nefasta* (AW08/09). Satin sandal with metal accessory.

115 *Quakan* (AW07/08). Green patent leather lace-up sandal.

116 *Bandir* (AW07/08). Vivid violet satin open-toed evening shoe, with tangerine leather lining and silk-velvet bow, on a teardrop heel.

117 *Salonica* (AW07/08). Trompe-l'oeil boot in pony and suede, with silk bow and grosgrain trim, on a teardrop heel.

118–19 *Fraseria* (SS06). Slingbacks in suede and satin with contrasting perforated soles; flat-fronted 'chopped' toe, on a raised 'footlift' and a painted wooden heel.

121 *Dubaia* (AW07/08). Silk-velvet shoe, decorated with baroque pearls held by glass beads, mother-of-pearl leaves and glass drops; limited edition for Dubai opening of Blahník store.

124 *Falu* (AW03/04). Printed pony bottine, with Lycra sock attached, on a red crocodile heel.

125 *Paglia* (SS05). Sandal with woven raffia and leather front and back, connected by strands of raffia and straw, held by elasticated leather, on a thread-covered heel.

126 *Galura* (SS09). Black leather court shoe with fishing-net detail inspired by Luchino Visconti's *La Terra Trema*.

127 *Trema* (SS03). Leather 'hammock net' shoe, with striped cotton lace-up back, on a painted heel.

128 *Caviara* (SS10). Cut-out boot in silk piqué, with grosgrain trim and satin lining, on a painted stacked heel.

129 *Ankole* (2005). Evening mule in powder blue suede, with silk braid and wooden beads, covered in macrame lace; scalloped lining.

130 *Pulque* (SS10). Flat cut-out thong in spotted linen with red leather lining and suede bows.

131 *Gloton* (SS10). Spotted Canepa linen court shoe with a raised flat front, on a painted wooden heel.

132 *Yati* (AW07/08). 'Stomacher' evening shoe in silk satin, with silk-velvet Mokuba bows; flat, 'chopped' front, on a teardrop heel.

133 *Kaisut* (SS05). D'Orsay shoe, in silk brocade by Lisio, with soft nappa 'curtain', trimmed with golden beads, all lined in electric blue velvet.

134 *Sedutta* (SS02). Coral silk-crêpe evening shoe, with anklets of real coral beads and drops.

135 *Panchal* (SS06). Dyed Roccia Lizard slingbacks, embroidered with irregular seed pearls on a flat-fronted 'chopped' toe.

136 Above: *Corbola* (AW06/07). Spotted silk-velvet shoe outlined with padded leather inserts.
Below: *Palikir* (AW06/07). Black satin court shoe, with cut-outs bordered in bronze leather with door-handle attachment.

special
thanks

First and foremost, I would like to thank everyone who worked with me on this book: the contributors, Ms Suzy Menkes, Ms Grace Coddington, Ms Amy Fine Collins, Carlos García-Calvo, Ms Milena Canonero, Michael Roberts, Bruce Weber and Nan Bush; and those who worked to make it possible: Thomas Neurath and Ms Constance Kaine at Thames & Hudson, Ms Teresa Roviras (who is now like family), my niece Kristina, Joe Fountain, everyone at Steidl, and the estates of Roloff Beny, Fyodor Dostoevsky and Federico García Lorca.

Throughout my career I have had the privilege to work with and come into contact with some truly wonderful people whom I would like to take this opportunity to thank.

The editors and the image makers of the publications who have been so instrumental in my trajectory: Ms Anna Wintour for her constant inspiration and support through the years; Ms Grace Coddington for the unfailing beauty of her imagery; Ms Alexandra Shulman for her divine mind; and her predecessor, the supremely generous Ms Beatrix Miller; Ms Franca Sozzani for her vision and excellent taste; Ms Carine Roitfeld for the excitement of her pages; Ms Yolanda Sacristan... Por España!, André Leon Talley, Ms Anna Harvey, Ms Julia Reed, Ms Sarah Jane Hoare, Ms Angelica Bleidschmid, Ms Christiane Arp, Ms Aliona Doletskaya, Ms Virginia Smith, Ms Candy Pratts Price, Ms Elissa Santisi, Ms Virginia Galvin, Ms Lourdes Garzon, Ms Nieves Fontana, Ms Patricia Field, Ms Carlyne Cerf de Dudzeele, Iain R. Webb, Ms Susannah Frankel, Colin McDowell, Ms Camilla Morton, Ms Carmen Borgonovo and Ms Mouchette Bell.

The friends and members of my family who have been there for me since the beginning: my darling sister Evangelina and, again, her daughter Kristina, Ms Paloma Picasso, Ms Bianca Jagger, Peter Schlesinger and Eric Boman, Peter Hinwood, Ms Min Hogg, David and Catherine Bailey, Ms Anna Piaggi, Jonathan and Ronnie Newhouse, Peter Young, Ms Nineveh Khomo and Delilah, Ms Chris Massingham, Betty and George Pochmann, Pierre Bergé, Stewart Grimshaw, Ms Joan Juliet Buck, Antoni Bernard, Ms Elsa Lopez, Ms Elsa Fernández Santos, Ms Maribel Arocha Lugo, Ms Petra Hartmann, Ms Silvia Alexandrovich, Ms Amanda Lear, Jasper Conran, Ms Grace Jones, Ms Natasha Fraser-Cavassoni, Walter Pfeiffer, Peter and Annie Frankel, Lolo and Jorge Lozano VandeWalle, the beautiful and marvellous Spanish actresses Ms Maribel Verdú, Ms Lolita Flores, Ms Paz Vega and Ms Angela Molina.

The designers: John Galliano, Azzedine Alaïa, Ms Carolina Herrera, Karl Lagerfeld, Antonio Berardi, Ms Donatella Versace, Oscar de la Renta, Calvin Klein, Jean-Paul Gaultier, Zac Posen, Ms Celia Birtwell, Paul Smith, Isaac Mizrahi, Domenico Dolce, Stefano Gabbana and Rifat Ozbek.

The most elegant women who have worn my shoes over the years in a way I would never have dreamt possible: HRH Doña Letizia, Princess of Asturias, HRH the Infanta Elena, Duchess of Lugo, Lady Amanda Harlech, Ms Lucy Birley, Ms Loulou de la Falaise, Ms Marisa Berenson, Ms Anjelica Huston, The Hon Daphne Guinness, Ms Yasmin Le Bon, Ms Tilda Swinton, Ms Kate Moss, Ms Naomi Campbell, Ms Marguerite Littman, Ms Jerry Hall, Ms Marie Helvin, Ms Tina Turner, Iman, Ms Kylie Minogue and Ms Sarah Jessica Parker, with gratitude.

To the people who work with me, turning what is drawn on paper into a reality, and getting them on to feet: in Milan, the families who run the factories; in London, everyone in the shop and office; in New York, George Malkemus, Tony Yurgaitis, everyone in our shop and office and the incomparable Mr Burt Tansky.

To everyone at Anderson & Sheppard.

To all those who, unfortunately, are no longer with us, but are forever in my thoughts: the late Mrs Diana Vreeland, my mentor; Ms Tina Chow, my best friend; Sir Cecil Beaton, Ms Liz Tilberis, Ossie Clark, Ms Alice Ormsby-Gore, Ms Chelita Secunda, Ms Isabella Blow, Simon Sainsbury, Guillermo Cabrera Infante, Gianni Versace, Perry Ellis, Irving Penn, Joseph Ettedgui and to the artist and true genius that was Mons Yves Saint Laurent.

And, most importantly, to all of the customers who have supported me and my work over the years.

Thank you

notes

'Ballad of the Moon, Moon'

The moon came to the forge
with her bustle of tuberoses.
The child looks at her, looks at her.
The child is looking at her.
In the shifting air
the moon moves her arms
and shows, brazen and pure,
her breasts of hard pewter.

'Run away, moon, moon, moon.
If the gypsies come,
they will make your heart
into white rings and necklaces.'

'Child, let me dance.
If the gypsies come,
they will find you on the anvil
with your little eyes closed.'

'Run away, moon, moon, moon.
I can feel their horses coming.'

'Child, leave me, do not step
on my starched whiteness.'

The rider moved closer,
hoofbeats drumming on the plain.
Inside the forge the child
keeps his eyes closed.

Through the olive trees they came,
bronze and dreamlike, the gypsies.
Their heads held high
and their eyes half shut.

How the nightjar sings,
oh, how it sings in the tree!
The moon moves through the sky
holding a child by the hand.

Inside the forge they weep,
crying out, the gypsies.
The air keeps vigil, vigil.
The air is keeping vigil.

FEDERICO GARCÍA LORCA

picture credits

6 © Michael Roberts/Maconochie Photography; 12 Photograph © Bruce Weber; 22 © Library and Archives Canada. Reproduced with the permission of Library and Archives Canada. Source: Library and Archives Canada/Credit: Roloff Beny/*A Time of Gods*, p. 67/Roloff Beny fonds; 38 © Library and Archives Canada. Reproduced with the permission of Library and Archives Canada. Source: Library and Archives Canada/Credit: Roloff Beny/*The Thrones of Earth and Heaven*, p. 122/Roloff Beny fonds; 46 © Library and Archives Canada. Reproduced with the permission of Library and Archives Canada. Source: Library and Archives Canada/Credit: Roloff Beny/*Pleasure of Ruins*, p. 106/Roloff Beny fonds; 62 © Library and Archives Canada. Reproduced with the permission of Library and Archives Canada. Source: Library and Archives Canada/Credit: Roloff Beny/*Pleasure of Ruins*, p. 3/Roloff Beny fonds; 74 Bridgeman/Getty Images; 86 © Library and Archives Canada. Reproduced with the permission of Library and Archives Canada. Source: Library and Archives Canada/Credit: Roloff Beny/*A Time of Gods*, p. 17/Roloff Beny fonds; 92 © Library and Archives Canada. Reproduced with the permission of Library and Archives Canada. Source: Library and Archives Canada/Credit: Roloff Beny/*A Time of Gods*, p. 62/Roloff Beny fonds; 98 akg-images/Erich Lessing; 108 © Michael Roberts/Maconochie Photography; 120 Imagesource/Getty Images; 140 © Library and Archives Canada. Reproduced with the permission of Library and Archives Canada. Source: Library and Archives Canada/Credit: Roloff Beny/*The Thrones of Earth and Heaven*, p. 102/Roloff Beny fonds; 150 Axiom Photographic Agency/Getty Images; 158 Brand X Pictures/Getty Images; 172 Marimekko's 'Mini-Unikko' fabric print by Maija and Kristina Isola; 184 Photodisc/Getty Images; 196 © Michael Roberts/Maconochie Photography; 198 Photograph by Manolo Blahník, © Manolo Blahník

sources of quotations

8 Federico García Lorca, 'Romance de la luna, luna', *Romancero Gitano*, 1921–27
149 Bernard Berenson, Cyrene, 16 April 1935, as quoted in Roloff Beny, *The Thrones of Earth and Heaven*, 1958, p. 101
157 Fyodor Dostoevsky, *The Adolescent*, 1875 (orginally published in 1916 in English by William Heinemann Ltd as *A Raw Youth*), English translation by Constance Garnett, p. 78

Library of Congress Cataloging-in-Publication Data
Blahnik, Manolo, 1942-
Manolo's new shoes : drawings by Manolo Blahník/by Manolo Blahník ; foreword by Suzy Menkes. — 1st ed.
p. cm.
ISBN 978-1-58093-282-0
1. Shoes—Pictorial works. 2. Fashion drawing. 3. Blahnik, Manolo, 1942- I. Title.
TT678.5B59 2010
741.6'72—dc22   2010015373

Book designed by Teresa Roviras

Printed and bound in Germany

10 9 8 7 6 5 4 3 2 1
First American Edition

www.monacellipress.com